CREATIVE SKILLET COOKING

Beryl Frank

WEATHERVANE
BOOKS

CREDITS

Presto
National Presto Industries
Eau Claire, Wisconsin 54701

Thanks to the husband who lived with a skillet instead of a wife for the duration of this book.

contents

introduction

The skillet is the most useful and most used pan in the kitchen. Whether you scramble eggs for breakfast, fry bacon for luncheon sandwiches, or cook hamburgers for dinner, the pan you use, in one form or another, is the skillet.

Almost every culture in the world has used a skillet for cooking. Museums have examples of skillets in their exhibits of homemaking tools. Wherever man or woman put a utensil on a fire to cook, you will find a form of skillet.

how to choose a skillet

If you are a novice cook just setting up housekeeping, shop around for your first skillet—find the kind you think will best suit your needs. Buy only one medium-size skillet first. Use it—then decide if it is the kind you like. Many people have purchased glamorous sets of skillets only to find that, for one reason or another, they don't like them. First, find one you like, then buy others as you need them.

kinds of skillets

cast-iron

The cast-iron skillet is the basic skillet used by cooks for generations. It is heavy in weight, heats evenly, and holds its heat well. When properly seasoned by years of wear, the cast-iron skillet looks black and cooks even better than when new. A really fine inheritance from Grandmother would be her cast-iron skillets. They are still made today in several different sizes, and domed glass lids are available. All the recipes in this book can be prepared successfully in a cast-iron skillet.

lightweight-steel and aluminum

Both these metals are light in weight. In an era of orthopedic problems, a lightweight skillet can be a help. They cook well, are easy to clean, and are useful for stir-frying in place of a wok.

enameled cast-iron

This type of skillet has devotees who swear by it. It is by far the most attractive looking, as it comes in many colors. It is also usually quite expensive. It does not have the sensitivity to temperature changes of the all-metal skillet. The enamel finish is "lovely to look at"—be sure it is for you when you buy.

glass, copper, and cast-aluminum

These all have some pluses and some minuses. The best way to know what will suit you is to shop around. Look at the skillet. Hold it in your hand. Ask questions, and, when you have answers that fill your cooking requirements, make your decision.

electric

These new appliances do not always replace the stove-top skillet, but they offer a new dimension in cooking at the table. Pancakes can be cooked with the family. Dinner can be prepared and kept warm on a constant, low electric heat. The cook can stay cool and comfortable and conserve energy at the same time. They are also attractive and very easy to clean.

If you have read this far, you know a variety of skillets is available for the modern homemaker. The cooking tools mean as much to a successful recipe as the recipe itself. All the recipes in this book will work well in the skillet you are comfortable using.

skillet shapes and sizes

Skillets come in many shapes and sizes. For this reason, the recipes in this book do *not* specify inches. Rather, the measure is large, medium, and small. A general rule to guide the cook is:

Large skillet — approximately 12 inches
Medium skillet — approximately 9 inches
Small skillet — approximately 6 inches

a final tip or two

In this book tomatoes are rarely peeled and seeded, as there are vitamins to be saved. If you prefer your recipes with peeled tomatoes, put them in boiling water for two minutes. They will then peel easily.

Experiment with spices. Discover a new taste by adding dill or sage to almost any entree or vegetable. Try lemon and pepper seasoning. Learn to use oregano. A new subtle flavor will enhance your overall cooking, and the new aromas that emanate from your kitchen will tempt all appetites.

As for margarine versus butter, if you only use "the high cost spread," by all means use it with the recipes included here. However, if you are accustomed to using margarine in your cooking, whether specifically stated or not, margarine may be used in place of butter.

Where oil is called for, this is again your choice. Clear liquid vegetable oil is fine, or you can melt your own by using solid vegetable shortening.

When deep fat is required for cooking, the exact amount is not usually stated. If you are using a small skillet, you will, of course, need less shortening than for the 12-inch size. Start with at least 2 inches of melted shortening in the skillet. In deep frying, it is important that the hot fat be deep enough to cover the food to be fried and to permit it to move freely in the pan.

Now, at last, you are ready. You have a handy skillet or two. You need a new taste discovery. Read on, and start cooking in your skillet. It's really fun.

swedish meatballs

Yield: 48 balls

1 pound ground beef
1/4 pound ground veal
1/4 pound ground pork
2 cups bread crumbs
1/2 cup milk
1 onion, diced fine
2 tablespoons butter

2 1/2 teaspoons salt
1/4 teaspoon pepper
2 teaspoons nutmeg
2 teaspoons paprika
1 teaspoon dry mustard
3 beaten eggs
4 tablespoons butter or margarine

Have the meat ground together twice.

Soak bread crumbs in milk. Add meat; mix.

Sauté onion in large skillet in 2 tablespoons butter.

Mix together seasonings, eggs, onion, and meat in a bowl. Mix well; form into 48 small balls.

Melt butter in skillet; brown meatballs on all sides. Remove and set aside to make the sauce.

sauce

1/4 teaspoon garlic
5 tablespoons butter
2 teaspoons tomato paste
1 teaspoon beef concentrate

2 cups bouillon or soup stock
1 teaspoon aromatic
    bitters (optional)
1 cup sour cream

Add garlic and 1 tablespoon butter to fat left in skillet. Blend in 4 more tablespoons butter, the tomato paste, beef concentrate, and stock. Add bitters here, if desired. Stir mixture over low heat until it thickens, then pour sauce into a lighted chafing dish. Stir in sour cream. Add meatballs to sauce, stirring once or twice to be sure all heats through.

The sauce may be poured into a casserole dish and heated in the oven, if preferred. This recipe improves if made one day ahead of time.

swedish meatballs

party drumsticks

This is delightful party food, easy to handle with fingers, and fun to serve.

Yield: 24 drumsticks

12 chicken wings	**¼ teaspoon cinnamon**
½ cup flour	**¼ teaspoon pepper**
1 teaspoon salt	**Fat for deep frying**
¾ teaspoon ginger	

The trick to this recipe is in dividing the chicken wings. Separate each wing at the joints. This will give you 3 pieces. Reserve wing tips for soup later.

Mix flour, salt, and seasonings well. Coat each chicken piece thoroughly. Drop floured chicken into deep fat. Fry them quickly until crisp and golden brown. Drain.

Serve them for a party with your favorite sweet-and-sour sauce or by themselves.

Party drumsticks can be made ahead, frozen, and reheated in a moderate oven.

teriyaki steak bits

teriyaki steak bits

Yield: 6 to 8 servings

½ cup soy sauce
1 clove garlic, chopped fine
1 teaspoon ground ginger
2 tablespoons sugar

2 tablespoons sherry wine
1½ pounds steak, cut into
1-inch cubes
2 or more tablespoons margarine

Combine soy sauce, spices, sugar, and wine to make a marinade. Marinate meat in this at least 1 hour. Drain meat, reserving liquid.

In a medium skillet, melt 2 tablespoons margarine. Brown meat cubes quickly on all sides. Place meat in a chafing dish; pour sauce over it. Stir occasionally. You won't have to stir much, as your guests will eat the steak on handy toothpicks very quickly. If you like, add some pineapple chunks to the chafing dish.

party liver pâté

party liver pâté

Yield: 10 to 16 servings

¼ pound butter or chicken fat
1 large onion, chopped fine
1 pound chicken livers

1 tablespoon Worcestershire sauce
Salt and pepper to taste

Melt butter or chicken fat in medium skillet; lightly tan chopped onion. Add chicken livers; cook until they are slightly pink at the center, about 5 minutes. Remove from heat.

Put entire mixture through a food mill so it is ground very smooth. If you use a colander instead of a food mill, you may want to put the liver mixture through twice to ensure a smooth texture. Last, add Worcestershire sauce and salt and pepper. Mix together well with a spoon.

Shape pâté into a greased mold for a party. Turn out on a serving plate and surround with party crackers so that guests may help themselves.

10

hot dogs in brandy

This can be made directly in a chafing dish or done in a skillet on the stove—your choice.

Yield: Never quite enough, as these are so popular

  ½ cup brown sugar
  ½ cup soy sauce
  ¼ cup brandy
  1 12-ounce package cocktail hot dogs

Mix sugar, soy sauce, and brandy until blended and hot—3 to 5 minutes. Add hot dogs; simmer together 10 minutes. Have toothpicks handy so that hot dogs can be removed from sauce to be eaten.

shrimp fritters

Yield: About 12 fritters

  ½ cup water
  2 tablespoons butter
  ½ cup flour
  2 eggs, well-beaten
  ½ cup grated cheese (American or Gruyère)
  1 cup diced cooked shrimp
  Fat for deep frying

Bring water and butter to a boil in a saucepan. Add flour all at once, stirring vigorously with a wooden spoon. Stir until mixture pulls away from sides of pan. Remove from heat. Add eggs. The mixture will be smooth and thick. Stir in shrimp and cheese.

Heat fat for deep frying in skillet. Drop mixture by teaspoonfuls into fat. Cook until evenly browned and crisp.

fish balls for a party

shrimp in garlic butter

Yield: 6 to 10 servings for a party

¼ **pound butter or margarine**	3 **tablespoons finely**
1 **garlic clove, cut in half**	**chopped parsley**
48 **jumbo shrimp, peeled**	½ **cup sherry**
and cleaned	

Melt butter in skillet and heat garlic halves 2 minutes. Remove garlic.

Add shrimp to butter and sauté for 5 minutes or until shrimp are pink. Remove to a hot platter or chafing dish.

Add parsley and sherry to the butter in the skillet; stir until hot, about 30 seconds.

Pour the sauce over the shrimp and watch them disappear.

fish balls for a party

Yield: 24 to 36 balls

2 pounds frozen haddock fillets
1 cup cracker meal
2 teaspoons salt
Dash of white pepper
1½ cups light cream
Fat for deep frying
Parsley and paprika for garnish

Put haddock, partially thawed, through a food grinder twice. Place it in a large bowl. Add cracker meal, salt, pepper, and cream. Mix until smooth.

Now, put your hands under cold water. With moist hands, shape fish mixture into 1-inch balls.

Heat fat in medium skillet; using a slotted spoon, drop fish balls into fat. Allow to simmer for 10 minutes. Remove cooked fish balls with slotted spoon; drain on paper towels. Cook rest of balls in same way.

Put fish balls on a heated platter and sprinkle with parsley and paprika. Keep toothpicks handy for picking up these delicacies.

salmon balls

These can be kept warm in an oven or on a hot plate for continual serving during a party evening.

Yield: 6 to 10 servings

1 15-ounce can salmon
1 egg, beaten
½ cup flour
½ cup freshly ground black pepper
1 heaping teaspoon baking powder
Fat for deep frying

Drain salmon and reserve liquid. Add egg to salmon, followed by flour and pepper.

Mix baking powder in ¼ cup salmon liquid and add to salmon mixture.

Heat fat in skillet. Drop salmon mixture by teaspoonfuls to form balls. Fry until golden brown and crusty.

Drain on paper towels; serve salmon balls at once.

cheese cubes

Yield: About 2 dozen

1½ cups bread crumbs mixed with ½ teaspoon dillweed
2 eggs, beaten
1 pound Swiss cheese, cut into 1-inch cubes
Fat for deep frying

Take 2 tablespoons from bread crumbs and beat with eggs. Put rest of crumbs in a pie plate. Dip cheese cubes into egg mixture, then into dry crumbs. Coat all over.

Heat shortening in medium skillet and drop breaded cheese into it, a few cubes at a time. Cook for 1 minute, until golden, then lift out. Drain on paper towels. Keep cubes warm until all are cooked, then pass the platter.

To make these successfully, be sure cheese cubes are well-battered in egg and crumbs, and work fast in the fryer. They're worth the trouble, though.

cheese cubes

sweet-potato fingers

Yield: About 4 servings

4 to 6 cooked sweet potatoes
¼ cup flour
Fat for deep frying

½ cup brown sugar
1 teaspoon salt
½ teaspoon nutmeg

Cut sweet potatoes into strips or fingers. Dip each finger into flour so it is well-coated.

Heat fat in medium skillet. Fry potato fingers until golden brown. Drain on paper towels. Sprinkle with a mixture of brown sugar, salt, and nutmeg.

Keep these tasty appetizers on a hot tray until party time. They'll go fast.

sweet-potato fingers

curried nuts

Yield: 2 cups

¼ cup olive oil
1 tablespoon curry powder
1 tablespoon Worcestershire sauce

1/8 teaspoon cayenne
2 cups nuts, assorted are best

Combine olive oil and seasonings in medium-size skillet. When mixture is hot, add nuts, stirring constantly until nuts are completely coated.

Line a baking pan with brown paper. Spread out nuts. Bake at 300°F for 10 minutes. The nuts should be crisp and tasty.

skillet popcorn

This is a nibble appetizer that all ages enjoy.

Yield: 1 large bowlful

3 tablespoons liquid shortening
½ cup corn for popping

Use a skillet with a tight-fitting lid for this. Heat shortening in medium skillet until one kernel of corn dropped in sizzles. Add corn; cover, keeping heat low. When corn begins to pop, shake skillet gently to prevent it from sticking. Keep skillet moving until there is no more sound of popping. Put popcorn in a large bowl.

garlic butter

½ teaspoon garlic salt
¼ cup melted butter

Melt garlic salt in melted butter. Pour over cooked corn; toss gently.

cinnamon butter

1 tablespoon cinnamon-sugar
¼ cup melted butter

Stir cinnamon-sugar into melted butter. Pour over cooked corn; toss gently.

low-cal bacon dip

This recipe slid into the book because you do fry bacon in a skillet. It is so good it's worth stretching a point to include.

Yield: 1 plus cups dip, 16 calories per tablespoon

2 slices bacon, diced fine
1 cup plain yogurt
3 tablespoons sweet relish
1 tablespoon grated cheese
1 tablespoon catsup

Cook bacon until crisp in a small skillet. Drain and set aside.
Combine rest of ingredients in a small bowl, beating until smooth. Fold in bacon. Chill mixture for several hours.
Set it out surrounded by fresh, raw vegetables. Guests will love it.

salted almonds

It takes just a few minutes to have your own salted almonds, and they are so good at a party. Everybody likes salted almonds.

Yield: 4 cups

> **2 tablespoons butter or margarine**
> **1 pound blanched almonds**
> **Generous sprinkling of salt, onion salt, or garlic salt**

Melt the butter in a medium-size skillet. Do not let the butter brown. Stir in the blanched almonds; let them cook over low heat. Stir from time to time, or shake the skillet. When the almonds are lightly browned, sprinkle them generously with salt. Drain them on brown paper for 3 minutes. Then put the almonds on fresh brown paper to drain off remaining butter.

If you enjoy the taste of other salts, sprinkle the almonds with onion or garlic salt for a variety. Any way you season them, they are going to be a hit.

biscuit sticks

Yield: About 36 sticks

> **1 recipe of your favorite biscuit dough or**
> **1 package prepared biscuits**
> **Salt to taste**
> **Fat for deep frying**
> **1 garlic clove**

Roll out the biscuit dough; cut it into sticks ½ inch high by ½ inch wide by 3 inches long. Sprinkle the sticks with salt.

Melt the fat in a medium size skillet; season it with the garlic clove. Leave the clove in until you smell it in the fat, then remove it. Drop the sticks, a few at a time, into the hot fat; brown them lightly.

These are best served and eaten warm.

skillet for breakfast

fried bananas

Yield: 4 to 6 servings

¼ cup flour
1 teaspoon cinnamon

6 bananas, sliced lengthwise
2 or more tablespoons shortening

Mix flour and cinnamon together; thoroughly coat each piece of banana with mixture. If bananas are very long, you may prefer to quarter them.

Heat shortening in medium skillet. Brown the floured bananas, slowly turning them once.

Remove bananas to a heated platter; sprinkle with sugar.

skillet bread

This is simple to mix, tricky to turn in the skillet, and so good dripping with melted butter and jelly.

Yield: 4 to 6 servings; 1 loaf

2 cups flour
4 teaspoons baking powder
2 teaspoons salt

1¼ cups milk
2 tablespoons butter or margarine

Mix dry ingredients in a bowl. Add milk; blend with a wooden spoon. This will make a biscuit-like, spongy texture.

Heat butter in medium-size skillet. Keep heat low. Spread butter around evenly. Pour in batter. Cook for 15 minutes or until underside is golden brown. Here's the tricky part. Lift with a large spatula and turn to cook the other side for 15 minutes more.

Turn bread out onto a round plate; serve at once.

Picture on opposite page: fried bananas

bacon and egg cake

bacon and egg cake

Yield: 4 servings

> ½ pound bacon
> 6 eggs
> 1 tablespoon flour
> ½ teaspoon salt
> ½ cup milk or cream
> 3 tablespoons finely cut chives

Cut each bacon slice in half. Fry lightly but not too crisp in large skillet. Drain and set aside. Remove all but about 1 tablespoon of bacon fat from skillet.

Combine eggs, flour, and salt in a bowl. Gradually add milk.

Over moderate heat, warm the fat in the skillet. Pour in egg mixture; turn heat down to low. Do not stir. Let eggs set firm. This will take about 20 minutes. When mixture is firm, remove from heat.

Arrange bacon slices and chives on top. Serve directly from the pan.

danish egg cake with sausage

To make this a party brunch, serve Danish pastries along with the egg cake. Sure to be a hit.

Yield: 6 servings

> 3 medium boiled potatoes, sliced
> 1 8-ounce can cocktail sausages
> 2 tablespoons butter or margarine
> 4 eggs
>
> ¼ cup cream
> Green pepper for garnish
> 1 or 2 tomatoes for garnish

Dice potatoes. Slice cocktail sausages into same bowl; set aside.

Melt butter in medium skillet; brown potatoes and sausages together. Add well-beaten eggs mixed with cream. Cook over slow heat until mixture sets firm in the center.

Turn egg cake out onto a hot platter. Garnish with green pepper and tomato wedges.

basket eggs

Yield: 6 servings

1½ pounds lean ground beef
1 small onion, chopped fine
2 tablespoons catsup
1 teaspoon salt
¼ teaspoon pepper

¼ cup milk
6 hard-cooked eggs, shelled
1 raw egg, beaten
⅔ cup corn-flake crumbs
Fat for deep frying

Mix ground beef with onion, catsup, salt, pepper, and milk. When well-blended, form into 6 balls. Shape each ball of meat around a hard-cooked egg to completely cover the egg, forming an oval shape. Brush each meatball with beaten egg, then roll each in crumbs until covered all over.

Melt fat in medium skillet to make a 2-inch depth. Fry meatballs, 3 at a time, until crispy brown. (You will not have to turn them if you use deep fat.) Drain and keep them hot until all are done.

To serve, cut each meatball in half lengthwise. The eggs will then be in the basket.

basket eggs

eggs scandinavian

Yield: 6 to 8 servings

6 eggs
3 tablespoons condensed milk
1 teaspoon salt
Dash of pepper
2 dill pickles, sliced or diced
2 tablespoons chives

2 tablespoons chopped dill
8 ounces Danish cheese, diced
3 tablespoons butter
2 tomatoes
1 extra tablespoon chives
   for garnish

In a bowl mix eggs with milk, salt, and pepper. Add pickles, chives, dill, and cheese.

Heat butter in a large skillet. Add egg mixture; cover. Simmer on low heat 10 minutes.

While eggs are cooking, wash, peel, and quarter tomatoes.

When egg mixture has set in the middle, place tomatoes on top for decoration. Sprinkle with chives. Serve at once.

eggs scandinavian

eggs italian

Delicious and different for that Sunday-morning brunch for the family.

Yield: 4 to 6 servings

    2 tablespoons butter or margarine
    1 tablespoon chopped onion
    1 tablespoon diced green pepper
    6 eggs
    1 cup tomato soup
    1/8 teaspoon salt

Melt the butter in a medium skillet. Add the onion and green pepper; cook over low heat for 3 minutes.

Stir the eggs, tomato soup, and salt in a bowl until well-blended. Pour into the skillet; cook until they are thick and creamy.

scrambled eggs with chicken

Yield: 4 to 6 servings

    8 eggs
    1 cup diced cooked chicken
    1 cup cream or milk
    1/2 teaspoon salt
    Dash of pepper
    2 tablespoons butter or margarine
    2 teaspoons chopped parsley or finely cut chives

Beat eggs slightly. Add chicken, cream, salt, and pepper.

Melt butter in medium skillet; add egg mixture. Stir lightly with a large spoon until eggs are firm and set.

Place eggs on a serving plate. Garnish with parsley or chives. Serve at once.

scrambled country corn

Yield: 4 to 6 servings

    6 slices lean bacon, diced
    1 medium onion, chopped
    1 green pepper, chopped
    2 cups corn kernels, fresh preferred,
        but canned may be used
    1 large tomato, chopped
    6 eggs
    1 teaspoon Worcestershire sauce
    1 teaspoon salt
    Dash of freshly ground pepper

In a deep skillet cook bacon until almost crisp. Pour off excess fat. Add onion, green pepper, corn, and tomato. Sauté until onion is transparent.

Beat eggs and seasonings in a bowl until light and frothy. Stir into the skillet vegetables. Continue to stir until eggs are set.

Serve with your favorite pan of sweet rolls.

cottage-cheese scrambled eggs

Yield: 4 to 6 servings

    6 eggs, beaten
    ¾ cup cottage cheese
    2 tablespoons milk
    1 tablespoon chopped chives
    1 teaspoon dill
    ½ teaspoon salt
    Dash of freshly ground black pepper
    2 tablespoons butter or margarine

In mixing bowl beat eggs with a wire whisk or fork. Add cottage cheese, milk, and seasonings.

Heat butter in medium skillet, keeping heat low. Add egg mixture. As it cooks, lift edges with a spatula to allow liquid to flow off the top. Do not stir, but continue until eggs are set on top. Turn skillet over to bring eggs out of pan onto the serving plate.

scrambled eggs with sour cream

The sour cream adds a richness that makes these far more than just "plain scrambled eggs."

Yield: 4 to 6 servings

2 tablespoons butter or margarine
8 to 10 eggs, beaten
½ cup sour cream
1 teaspoon salt
¼ teaspoon freshly ground pepper

Melt butter in large skillet. It should just bubble, not brown.
In a bowl beat eggs until frothy. Add sour cream, salt, and pepper. Blend all together. Pour this mixture into skillet. Scramble mixture until eggs reach desired firmness.

scramburger for brunch

Yield: 4 to 6 servings

1 tablespoon oil
½ pound lean ground beef
1 small onion, finely chopped
8 eggs
½ cup milk
1 teaspoon salt
¼ teaspoon freshly ground black pepper

Heat oil in large skillet; brown ground beef and onion together.
In a bowl beat eggs, milk, salt, and pepper until light and frothy. Pour this over meat. Do not rush this. Cook it slowly and stir gently until eggs are firm.
Split and toast some bagels or English muffins to go with this.

danish omelet with herring

Yield: 4 to 6 servings

> 7-ounce can herring fillets or
>> 1 jar herring in sour cream
> Radishes, washed and sliced thin
> 6 to 8 eggs
> 3 tablespoons light cream
> 1 teaspoon salt
> ½ teaspoon lemon pepper
> 4 tablespoons butter or margarine
> Parsley for garnish

Cut herring into strips. If you prefer the herring in sour cream, cut it into 1-inch pieces.

Slice radishes and set aside. These must be ready first.

Beat eggs in a bowl with cream and seasonings.

Heat butter in a large skillet. Pour in eggs and allow to set lightly on the bottom. Tilt pan and let liquid run to sides. When eggs are set firm, slide omelet onto a heated platter.

Top the omelet with herring pieces, radishes, and parsley. Serve with your favorite hard rolls.

potato omelet

Yield: 4 to 6 servings

> 2 large potatoes, peeled and chopped fine
> 1 medium onion, chopped fine
> 1 teaspoon salt
> 5 tablespoons oil
> 6 eggs, beaten
> ⅓ cup milk
> Parsley for garnish

Cook potatoes and onion with salt in 3 tablespoons oil. Use a medium skillet. Cook about 5 minutes. Remove from heat.

Combine eggs and milk in a bowl. Add potato mixture to this.

Heat 2 more tablespoons oil in same skillet. Pour in egg mixture; reduce heat to low. Omelet will be nearly set in about 10 minutes. Turn and cook until the underside is firm. Garnish with parsley, if desired.

strawberry omelet

Yield: 4 to 6 servings

> 2 cups frozen whole strawberries
> 1 tablespoon sugar
> 4 eggs, separated
> ½ teaspoon salt
> 1 tablespoon lemon juice
> 1 tablespoon butter or margarine

Sprinkle strawberries with sugar; let stand for 2 hours to thaw.

Beat egg whites until you can turn the bowl upside down and they don't fall out. That's Grandmother's way of saying beat egg whites stiff.

Beat egg yolks with salt and lemon juice. Fold this into stiffly beaten egg whites until no yellow streaks remain.

Melt butter in medium skillet that can go into oven. Pour in egg mixture and tilt pan to coat sides. Cook over low heat just 5 minutes. When mixture is set on the bottom, bake at 350°F for 5 minutes more.

Lift omelet onto a heated plate and spoon strawberry mixture over it. Cut in pie wedges to serve.

cinnamon french toast

Yield: 4 servings

> 3 eggs, beaten slightly
> 1 teaspoon sugar
> 1 teaspoon cinnamon (more, if you prefer)
> 1 teaspoon salt
> 1 cup milk
> 10 slices slightly stale white bread
> 1 tablespoon butter or margarine

Break eggs into a pie plate; stir in sugar, cinnamon, salt, and milk. Dip each bread slice into this mixture as you are ready to put it in the skillet. Be sure bread absorbs on both sides.

Heat butter in medium skillet. Put in 1 slice of soaked bread. When bottom side is golden, turn it. Remove cooked toast to a warming platter.

Serve French toast with your favorite syrup or thick jam.

hawaiian french toast

Yield: 4 servings

2 eggs, beaten
1 cup pineapple juice
½ teaspoon salt

8 slices bacon, cooked and set aside
6 to 8 slices bread (day old is better)
Drained pineapple slices

Combine eggs, pineapple juice, and salt. This will be the liquid in which you soak each piece of bread.

Cook bacon crisp in medium skillet, drain it, and set aside, reserving fat.

Soak each piece of bread in the liquid. Fry it quickly on both sides in bacon drippings. Put it on a heated platter.

Garnish with bacon strips and a slice of pineapple. A real treat from the islands.

cheese fritters

If you want these for appetizers, make them smaller. Drop by teaspoons into hot fat. Good for a party.

Yield: About 20 fritters

1 egg, beaten
½ cup milk
1 teaspoon Worcestershire sauce
1 small onion, minced fine
Dash of hot pepper (optional)

2 cups biscuit mix
1½ cups diced American cheese
Fat for deep frying
Jelly or jam of your choice

In a bowl mix egg, milk, Worcestershire sauce, onion, pepper, and prepared biscuit mix. Blend well, then stir in the cheese.

Preheat fat in skillet. Drop mixture by tablespoons into hot fat. Fry until golden-brown fritters. Drain on paper towels.

Serve with your favorite jelly or jam.

corn fritters

Yield: About 12 fritters

2 eggs, separated
2 cups corn cut off the cob
½ teaspoon salt

¼ teaspoon pepper
¼ cup flour
¼ cup or more shortening

Separate egg yolks from whites; beat whites stiff.

Put corn in a mixing bowl. Add beaten egg yolks, salt, pepper, and flour. Mix well with a wooden spoon or rubber spatula. Gently fold in beaten egg whites.

Heat shortening. Drop fritters by spoonfuls into hot fat. When browned on both sides, drain on paper towels, then put onto a heated platter.

Serve as part of a brunch buffet.

apple fritters

Yield: 4 to 6 servings

> **4 to 6 apples, peeled and cored**
> **Wine to cover**

Cut the apples crosswise into ½-inch slices. Each slice will have a hole in the center. Soak the slices in wine for 2 hours.

fritter batter

> **2 egg yolks**
> **⅔ cup milk**
> **1 tablespoon lemon juice**
> **1 tablespoon melted butter**
> **1 cup flour**
>
> **¼ teaspoon salt**
> **2 tablespoons sugar**
> **2 egg whites, beaten stiff**
>
> **Deep fat for frying**

Combine the fritter batter ingredients in the order given by stirring them with a wooden spoon. Fold in the egg whites last.

Heat the fat in a large skillet.

Drain the apple slices, then dip them singly in the fritter batter. Fry them until lightly browned all over. Drain on a paper towel.

Serve the fritters piping hot.

pineapple fritters

Yield: 4 to 6 servings

fritter batter

> **2 egg yolks**
> **⅔ cup milk**
> **1 tablespoon lemon juice**
> **1 tablespoon melted butter**
> **1 cup flour**
> **¼ teaspoon salt**
> **2 egg whites, beaten stiff**
>
> **Deep fat for frying**
> **1 large can pineapple slices, drained**
> **Confectioners' sugar**

With a wooden spoon, stir the fritter batter ingredients in the order given. Fold in the egg whites last.

Heat the fat for deep frying in a large skillet. Dip each pineapple ring in the batter, coating it thoroughly. Fry until lightly browned all over. Drain fritters on a paper towel.

Sprinkle fritters with confectioners' sugar, if desired. Serve.

johnnycake

This is a change from pancakes and is full of history. American colonists made Johnnycake out of Indian cornmeal.

Yield: 12 4-inch cakes

    1 cup yellow or white cornmeal
    ½ teaspoon salt
    2 teaspoons sugar
    1 cup water
    2 tablespoons butter or margarine
    ¼ cup milk
    Margarine and oil for frying

Put cornmeal, salt, and sugar into a mixing bowl.

Heat water and 2 tablespoons butter in a saucepan. Bring to rolling boil.

Slowly pour this hot liquid into cornmeal, stirring constantly. When all liquid has been absorbed, add milk. This will be a thick batter.

Heat margarine and oil in skillet—enough to cover entire cooking surface generously. Drop batter by tablespoons into skillet, to form 4-inch cakes. Cook until golden brown, then turn to brown the other side.

Serve at once with maple syrup.

hawaiian pancakes

Don't really know if Hawaiians ever made these or not, but they are delicious.

Yield: 14 to 16 pancakes

    1 cup milk
    1 egg
    1 tablespoon shortening
    1 cup prepared pancake mix
    1 can crushed pineapple, drained

Add milk, egg, and melted shortening to prepared mix. Stir with a wooden spoon until batter is fairly smooth. Add pineapple.

Pour batter onto a hot, lightly greased skillet or griddle. When pancake is lightly brown around edges, turn once. Put cooked pancakes on a heated plate until all are done.

Serve with pineapple preserves, if desired.

mexican pancakes

These are a little trouble but are awfully good for dessert.

Yield: 4 to 6 servings

3 cups flour
1 tablespoon sugar
1 teaspoon baking powder
1 teaspoon salt
4 eggs

1 cup milk
4 tablespoons melted butter or margarine
¼ cup cold water
Fat for deep frying
Golden thick honey

Mix dry ingredients in a large bowl. Add eggs, milk, and butter, stirring well after each addition. Add cold water 1 tablespoon at a time until dough can be kneaded easily.

Turn dough onto a floured board; knead several times. Then divide dough into 2-inch balls; cover and let stand for 20 minutes.

Roll out each ball into a thin, round pancake. Let stand 5 minutes more.

Heat oil in medium skillet; fry pancakes a few at a time. When golden brown, drain on paper towels and keep them warm.

Serve covered with thick honey.

ham and cheese divine

Yield: 4 to 6 servings

½ cup chopped cooked ham
2 tablespoons butter or margarine
1 small onion, chopped fine
1 green pepper, diced
1 teaspoon prepared mustard
1 10½-ounce can condensed cheddar-cheese soup
¼ cup beer or sherry (milk, if preferred)
1 cup grated Swiss cheese
Freshly buttered toast

In a medium skillet lightly sauté ham in butter. Add onion and pepper; cook until onion is transparent. Add mustard, soup, and liquid; stir. You will have to stay with this dish. When mixture is smooth and hot, add grated cheese.

Spoon blended mixture over buttered toast. It's ready for healthy appetites.

rice pancakes

Yield: About 6 servings

    4 tablespoons butter, melted
    3 whole eggs, beaten
    2 cups cooked rice
    2 teaspoons baking powder
    1 teaspoon salt
    1 cup flour
    ¼ cup milk or cream
    Shortening for frying

rice pancakes

Mix ingredients in order given, adding milk to batter last.

Heat shortening in skillet. Drop by tablespoons into hot fat. When golden brown on one side, turn pancake. Add extra shortening if needed.

Serve rice pancakes with apricot preserves.

dollar nut pancakes

dollar nut pancakes

Make these pancakes small—about the size of a silver dollar. They're a little more trouble to make, but they do add to a brunch spread.

Yield: 16 to 24 pancakes

> 1½ **cups flour**
> 2 **tablespoons sugar**
> 1 **tablespoon baking powder**
> ½ **teaspoon salt**
> 1 **egg, beaten**
> 1½ **cups milk**
> ¼ **cup chopped nuts**
> **Fat for frying**

Mix ingredients in order given, beating in nuts after all else is smooth.

Drop by teaspoons onto hot skillet or griddle. When pancake top is covered with bubbles and edges are firm, turn to brown the other side. Store on a hot platter until ready to bring to the table.

sourdough pancakes

This is a two-part operation. Start the night before.
These take a little longer than regular pancakes, but they are worth it.

Yield: 4 servings

> ½ **cup sourdough starter**
> 1 **cup evaporated milk**
> 1 **cup warm water**
> 2 **cups flour**
> 2 **eggs**
> 2 **tablespoons sugar**
> ½ **teaspoon salt**
> 1 **teaspoon soda**
> 2 **tablespoons oil**

Mix sourdough starter, milk, water, and flour in a bowl. Blend; leave at room temperature overnight.

Next morning, add rest of ingredients (except oil); mix, but do not beat. Use a wooden spoon for this.

Heat oil in skillet. Put in enough batter to make pancakes the size you prefer. Turn pancakes, and, when done, place on a warmed platter.

fried ham and potato cakes

Yield: 4 servings

    1 cup mashed potatoes (instant will do)
    1 cup finely diced cooked ham
    1 tablespoon chopped parsley
    ½ teaspoon onion salt
    ¼ teaspoon pepper
    Flour
    3 tablespoons oil for frying

Mix potatoes, ham, parsley, and seasonings. This mixture will be able to be shaped into flat cakes. Dip each cake into flour, being sure to batter both sides.

Heat oil in skillet. Sauté cakes in oil, adding more oil if needed. When cakes are browned on both sides, set on a warm platter until ready to serve.

rarebit for brunch

Yield: 4 to 6 servings

    2 tablespoons butter or margarine
    2 tablespoons flour
    ¾ cup milk
    ⅛ teaspoon baking soda
    1 1-pound can tomatoes, drained
    1½ cups shredded Cheddar cheese
    ½ teaspoon dry mustard
    ½ teaspoon salt
    6 buttered, toasted English muffins, split open

Melt butter in a medium-sized, heavy skillet. Stir in flour and remove from heat.

Gradually add milk to make a smooth, thick paste. Return to low heat.

Mix baking soda with tomatoes; add to skillet. Gradually add remaining ingredients (except muffins), stirring over low heat until all cheese melts.

Spoon this mixture over English muffins; serve.

tomato rarebit

Yield: 4 servings

　　1½ cups tomato puree
　　1 cup diced American cheese
　　1 beaten egg
　　½ teaspoon salt
　　2 teaspoons brown sugar

Use a heavy medium-size iron skillet for this and low heat all the way.

Heat the tomato puree and cheese together until the cheese is melted and mixed. Add the beaten egg; stir until slightly thickened. Last, add salt and brown sugar; stir to blend.

Serve the rarebit over hot toast.

meat

beef burgundy

Yield: 4 to 6 servings

4 tablespoons oil
4 or 5 medium onions, sliced
2 pounds lean beef, cut into
    1-inch cubes
1½ tablespoons flour
½ teaspoon marjoram or thyme
    (if you like both flavors, use
    ¼ teaspoon of each)

1 teaspoon salt
½ teaspoon pepper
½ cup bouillon
1 cup dry red wine
½ pound fresh mushrooms, sliced

Heat oil in large, heavy skillet. Cook onions until transparent. Remove onions; set aside.

Sauté beef cubes until brown. Sprinkle browned meat with flour and seasonings. Add bouillon and wine; simmer slowly until meat is tender, about 1½ hours. Add more liquid if needed to keep beef covered (1 part bouillon to 2 parts wine).

When meat is tender, add onions and mushrooms; cook about 30 minutes more, stirring occasionally. The sauce will be thick and delicious.

beef chinese

Yield: 4 to 6 servings

1 7-ounce package frozen
    Chinese pea pods
3 tablespoons oil
1 pound beef tenderloin tips, sliced
    thin across grain
½ cup chopped onion

1 small garlic clove, minced fine
4 cups sliced raw cauliflower florets
1 cup beef broth
2 tablespoons cornstarch
¼ cup soy sauce
½ cup water

Separate pea pods by pouring boiling water over them. Drain at once.

Heat 2 tablespoons oil in skillet. Add half the beef; brown quickly. Remove cooked beef, allow skillet to heat again, and brown rest of meat. Remove from skillet.

Add remaining tablespoon of oil; sauté onion and garlic 1 minute. Add cauliflower and beef broth. Cook just 3 minutes.

Mix cornstarch, soy sauce, and water; stir into skillet. Add beef and pea pods; stir until sauce thickens.

Serve at once over rice.

hungarian goulash

Yield: 4 to 6 servings

2 pounds lean stewing beef, cut into 1-inch cubes
5 tablespoons flour
1 tablespoon fat or bacon drippings
2½ cups tomato juice

1 small onion, diced
1 tablespoon Worcestershire sauce
2 teaspoons salt
1 teaspoon paprika
¼ teaspoon pepper
½ cup sour cream

Dredge meat cubes generously with flour.

Melt fat in large skillet. Brown meat on all sides. Add tomato juice, onion, and seasonings. Bring to a boil, then reduce heat. Cover skillet; simmer for 1 hour or until meat is tender.

When ready to serve, stir in sour cream; simmer just 2 minutes. Hot broad noodles go well with this goulash.

beef round over noodles

Yield: 4 to 6 servings

2 tablespoons shortening
1 teaspoon soy sauce
½ teaspoon sugar
2 teaspoons sherry
3 cups thinly sliced onions
2 teaspoons cornstarch
1 tablespoon soy sauce
1½ pounds beef round, cut into 1-inch pieces
1 tablespoon Worcestershire sauce
1 teaspoon garlic salt
1 can mushrooms (optional)

beef round over noodles

Heat shortening in large skillet with 1 teaspoon soy sauce, sugar, and 1 teaspoon sherry. Sauté onions in this.

Mix cornstarch, 1 tablespoon soy sauce, and 1 teaspoon sherry in a bowl. Dredge meat in this mixture, coating every piece.

Put dredged meat in onion mixture; brown it. Stir in Worcestershire sauce and garlic salt. Cover skillet; let simmer for 1 hour. This meat draws its own gravy, but you may want to stir occasionally while it cooks.

Serve on a bed of noodles and enjoy.

beef in sour cream

Yield: 4 to 6 servings

> 2 pounds beef round, cut into 1-inch pieces
> 2 tablespoons lemon juice
> 2 tablespoons flour
> 2 tablespoons butter or margarine
> 1 tablespoon oil
> 1 large onion, sliced thin
> 1 clove garlic, minced
> 1½ cups beef broth
> 1 teaspoon salt
> Dash of pepper
> 1 package frozen peas, thawed
> 1 cup sour cream
> 2 tomatoes, diced

Sprinkle meat with lemon juice, then flour. Allow to stand for 10 minutes.

Heat butter and oil in large skillet; brown the meat. Add onion, garlic, beef broth, salt, and pepper; cover. Cook over low heat 1 hour or until meat is fork-tender. This may be done in the morning and reheated at mealtime.

Just before serving, add thawed peas, sour cream, and tomatoes. Allow this to get hot over low heat, then serve at once. Noodles go well.

sweet-and-sour beef

Yield: 6 to 8 servings

> 1 tablespoon shortening
> 2 pounds cubed lean stewing beef
> ½ teaspoon salt
> 2 cups canned tomatoes
> ⅓ cup brown sugar

> ⅓ cup vinegar
> ½ cup finely chopped onion
> ½ bay leaf
> 1 green pepper, cut into thin strips

Melt shortening in large skillet; brown beef on all sides. Add salt, tomatoes, brown sugar, vinegar, onion, and bay leaf. Cover skillet; lower heat. Allow to simmer about 2 hours or until beef is tender.

Last, add pepper strips to beef; cook for 10 minutes more to blend all flavors. Serve over hot rice or with noodles.

Picture on opposite page: sweet-and-sour beef

swiss steak in sour cream

Yield: 4 servings

  1½- to 2-pound round steak, 1 inch thick
  ¼ cup flour
  1 teaspoon salt
  ¼ teaspoon pepper
  2 tablespoons oil
  2 medium onions, sliced
  ½ cup water
  ½ cup sour cream
  2 tablespoons grated cheese
  Paprika to taste

Dredge round steak on both sides with flour seasoned with salt and pepper.
Heat oil in large skillet. Brown the steak well. Add remaining ingredients; cover skillet. Simmer for 1 hour or until meat is tender to the fork.

pepper steak

Yield: 4 to 6 servings

  1½ pounds boneless steak,
     cut into thin strips
  ½ cup chopped onions
  3 tablespoons salad oil
  2 cups beef bouillon
  1 can water chestnuts, sliced
  1 can mushrooms
  2 green peppers, sliced
  1 can pineapple tidbits (optional)
  2 tablespoons cornstarch
  2 tablespoons soy sauce
  ½ cup water
  Salt and pepper to taste

Brown the meat and onions in hot oil in large skillet. Gradually stir in bouillon; simmer until meat is tender. Add water chestnuts, mushrooms, and peppers. If using pineapple, drain and add it, too. Simmer for 5 minutes.

Blend cornstarch with soy sauce and water. Add to meat; stir constantly until slightly thickened. Season with salt and pepper.

This is especially good served on a bed of hot rice.

round steak in beer

Yield: 4 to 6 servings

 1½ pounds round steak, cut in 1-inch cubes
 4 tablespoons butter or margarine
 ½ cup minced chives or chopped onion
 1 bay leaf
 ½ teaspoon thyme
 1 teaspoon salt
 Pepper to taste
 2 cups beer
 1 tablespoon cornstarch
 ¼ cup water

Brown steak cubes in heated butter in medium skillet. Add chives, spices, and beer. Cover; cook over medium heat 1 hour or until meat is tender. Add extra seasonings, if desired.

Mix cornstarch with water to form a paste; add to skillet. Stir until gravy thickens slightly, then serve.

beef barbecue

Yield: 4 to 6 servings

 1½ pounds lean ground beef
 2 tablespoons shortening
 1 onion, chopped
 1 green pepper, diced
 ½ cup catsup plus ½ cup water
 2 tablespoons brown sugar
 1 tablespoon Worcestershire sauce
 1 tablespoon prepared mustard
 1 teaspoon salt

Sauté ground beef in shortening in medium skillet about 10 minutes or until brown. Remove from skillet.

Put onion and green pepper in same shortening, cooking until onion is yellow and soft. Replace ground beef.

Mix together rest of ingredients; add to skillet. Stir to mix; simmer about 10 minutes.

Serve over hamburger rolls.

camper's chili

Because this is a one-pot dish, it works well when camping out, and it tastes good, too.

Yield: 4 to 6 servings

    1 tablespoon shortening
    1 pound lean ground beef
    1 large onion, chopped
    1 green pepper, chopped
    1 tablespoon chili powder
    1 can tomato soup
    2 cans red kidney beans, undrained

Heat shortening in medium skillet. Brown the ground beef with onion and green pepper. When all meat is browned, add chili powder, tomato soup, and kidney beans. Simmer for 10 to 15 minutes, stirring occasionally.
Serve on hamburger buns.

beef and pepper rice skillet

This quick-and-easy dish allows you to make a salad while the main dish is cooking; set the table, and eat—a favorite with busy people.

Yield: 4 to 6 servings

    1 pound ground beef
    2 green peppers, chopped
    1 cup sliced onion
    1 cup uncooked rice
    1 10½-ounce can beef broth
    1 10½-can water
    1 tablespoon soy sauce

Brown the beef in medium skillet. Stir in peppers, onion, rice, liquids, and soy sauce. Allow mixture to come to a boil. Reduce heat, stir once, and cover. Simmer about 25 minutes. Serve at once.

gumbo ground beef

Yield: 4 to 6 servings

  1 large onion, sliced
  1 tablespoon shortening
  1½ pounds ground beef
  1 can chicken-gumbo soup (condensed)
  1 teaspoon salt
  ¼ teaspoon freshly ground black pepper

Tan the onion in hot shortening in medium skillet. Add ground beef; stir until all is browned. Add can of soup—as is, without any extra water—and salt and pepper. Simmer about 5 minutes or until all flavors blend.

Serve on hamburger rolls.

swedish meatballs

Yield: 6 to 8 servings

  1 medium onion, finely chopped
  3 tablespoons butter
  1 cup mashed potatoes
  3 tablespoons bread crumbs
  1 pound lean ground beef
  ⅓ cup heavy cream

  1 teaspoon salt
  1 egg
  1 tablespoon chopped parsley (optional)
  2 tablespoons vegetable oil

Cook onion in 1 tablespoon butter until soft but not brown.

Combine onion, mashed potatoes, bread crumbs, meat, heavy cream, salt, egg, and parsley in a large bowl. Mix with a wooden spoon until well-blended. Shape into balls. Put on a flat tray and chill at least 1 hour before cooking.

Melt remaining butter and oil in large skillet. Fry meatballs on all sides until done through, about 8 to 10 minutes. Add more butter and oil, if needed. Transfer finished meatballs to casserole or baking dish; keep them warm.

sauce

  1 tablespoon flour
  ¾ cup light or heavy cream

Remove fat from skillet. On low heat stir in flour and cream. Stir constantly as sauce comes to a boil and becomes thick and smooth.

Pour sauce over the meatballs. Serve with broad noodles.

gingersnap meatballs

gingersnap meatballs

Yield: 4 to 6 servings

    1 pound lean ground beef
    ¾ cup bread crumbs
    1 medium onion, minced fine
    2 teaspoons salt
    ¼ teaspoon black pepper
    6 tablespoons lemon juice
    2 tablespoons water
    4 tablespoons margarine or shortening
    2½ cups beef broth
    ½ cup brown sugar
    ¾ cup gingersnap crumbs

Mix ground meat, bread crumbs, onion, salt, pepper, 3 tablespoons lemon juice, and water in a bowl. Mix well; form into 1-inch balls.

Heat shortening in medium skillet; brown the meatballs. Remove balls from pan.

Add beef broth and 3 tablespoons lemon juice to pan drippings. Bring to a boil, then add brown sugar and gingersnap crumbs. Add meatballs to this sauce and cook, covered, for 10 minutes. Stir once; allow to simmer uncovered 5 more minutes.

This goes well with noodles.

44

meat loaf skillet-style

Yield: 4 to 6 servings

> 1 pound lean ground beef
> 1 large onion, chopped
> 1 egg
> 2 tablespoons catsup
> 2 teaspoons chopped parsley
> 1 teaspoon salt
> ½ teaspoon black pepper
> 1 8-ounce can tomato sauce
> 1 can red kidney beans

Mix ground beef, onion, egg, catsup, parsley, salt, and pepper in a bowl. Shape meat mixture into a round loaf that will fit into your skillet. This can be done ahead and frozen, then thawed when ready to cook.

Place meat loaf into skillet and flatten it down to fit.

Mix tomato sauce and beans; pour over meat. Allow to simmer, covered, for 20 minutes. Uncover skillet; cook for 15 minutes more.

Cut meat loaf in wedges to serve.

sweet-and-pungent ham

Yield: 4 to 6 servings

> 1 green pepper, cut into
>   1-inch pieces
> ¼ cup vinegar
> ¼ cup brown sugar
> 1 cup water
> 1 tablespoon molasses
> 1 fresh tomato, diced
>
> 2 tablespoons cornstarch
> 1 teaspoon salt
> ¼ teaspoon pepper
> 1 cup canned pineapple cubes
>   (use pineapple liquid in place
>   of water, if desired)
> 2 to 3 cups diced cooked ham

Place green pepper, vinegar, sugar, ¾ cup water, and molasses into medium skillet. Stir until this boils. Add tomato pieces.

Mix cornstarch with remaining ¼ cup water; stir into sauce. Cook until mixture thickens. Add seasonings, pineapple cubes, and ham. Heat through, stirring very gently.

hash in a hurry

Yield: 4 to 6 servings

1 can condensed mushroom soup
¼ cup milk
1 cup cubed, cooked ham or other
    leftover meat

2 sliced hard-cooked eggs
Salt and pepper to taste
Triangles of toast

Mix soup and milk in a medium skillet, until well-blended. Add ham, egg slices, and seasonings. Heat this mixture over very low heat until all is blended.
Spoon the mixture over toast triangles. Serve.

ham leftovers delish

These are sure to go fast because they are so good.

Yield: 4 to 6 servings

1 cup mashed potatoes
1 cup ground cooked ham
¼ teaspoon lemon pepper

Flour for batter
2 or more tablespoons fat
    for frying

Mix mashed potatoes, ham, and lemon pepper together. Form into flat cakes about 3 inches in diameter. Dip each cake lightly in the flour; set aside.
Melt the fat in a medium skillet. Lightly brown each cake on both sides. These ham cakes may be kept warm in the oven until ready to serve all of them.

pan-fried liver and peppers

Yield: 4 servings

2 tablespoons butter or margarine
3 large green peppers, cut in ½-inch strips
4 slices calves' liver, ½ inch thick
2 tablespoons flour

1 teaspoon salt
1 teaspoon paprika
1 teaspoon lemon juice
Green pepper strips for garnish

Heat butter in large skillet. Cook pepper strips until tender, about 10 minutes. Remove peppers from skillet to platter to keep them warm.
Mix flour, salt, and paprika on waxed paper. Coat each liver slice with this mixture.
Place floured liver slices in same skillet, adding more butter if needed. Cook until crisp and brown on the outside—2 to 4 minutes per side.
Sprinkle cooked liver with lemon juice. Serve surrounded by pepper strips.

pan-fried lamb slices

Yield: 8 to 10 servings

1 leg of lamb
2 or 3 medium onions

Butter or vegetable shortening
Salt and pepper to taste

With a sharp knife cut lamb into ½-inch slices.

Peel and slice onions into rings; brown onions in butter in large skillet. Drain onions and set aside to keep warm.

In same shortening, fry meat slices; season with salt and pepper.

To serve, arrange meat on a platter. Cover slices with drained onions. Serve with mashed potatoes and a salad.

pan-fried lamb slices

lamb in grape sauce

Yield: 4 servings

   1½ pounds uncooked lamb, diced
   2 tablespoons oil or margarine
   ½ cup grape jelly or jam
   1 teaspoon dry mustard mixed with 1 teaspoon water
   1 teaspoon grated orange peel
   1 can prepared beef gravy
   1 tablespoon bourbon or brandy (optional)

Sauté lamb in hot oil in medium skillet. Lower heat to simmer. Add grape jelly and mustard. When these are forming a sauce, add remaining ingredients, stirring constantly. Cover; cook over low heat 25 minutes more.

This is delicious served with rice and a salad.

leftover lamb curry

Yield: 4 to 6 servings

   1 small chopped onion
   1 cup diced celery
   1 tablespoon oil
   1 tablespoon flour
   1 teaspoon curry powder
   2 cups beef broth
   ¼ cup catsup
   ½ teaspoon salt
   2 cups diced cooked lamb
   ½ cup chopped apple with skin for color

In medium skillet brown onion and celery in oil 3 minutes. With these, mix flour and curry powder, blending until smooth. Add beef broth, catsup, and salt. Let simmer about 1 hour, stirring occasionally.

Last, add cooked lamb and chopped apple; continue to simmer for 20 minutes more.

Serve the lamb curry over rice.

lamb lovely

Yield: 4 to 6 servings

2 cups diced cold cooked lamb
2 hard-cooked eggs, riced or chopped fine
2 tablespoons oil
1 tablespoon lemon juice
2 tablespoons butter

3 tablespoons flour
1 teaspoon dry mustard
2 cups stock (lamb or beef will do)
1 teaspoon Worcestershire sauce
1 teaspoon salt

Combine the lamb, eggs, oil, and lemon juice in a bowl.
Melt the butter in a medium-size skillet.
Blend the flour and mustard to make a paste. Gradually stir in the stock. Add Worcestershire and salt; stir until the sauce comes to a boil. It will thicken slightly. Last, add the lamb and egg mixture; heat thoroughly.
Serve the lamb over rice or on toast points.

sweet-and-sour lamb chops

Yield: 4 servings

4 lean lamb chops, 1 inch thick
    (shoulder chops will do)
1 13-ounce can pineapple chunks
¼ cup soy sauce
¼ cup vinegar
½ teaspoon dry mustard
1 tablespoon oil
¼ cup brown sugar
1 teaspoon cornstarch

Put chops in the bowl for the marinade.
Drain pineapple chunks; reserve liquid.
Combine pineapple liquid with soy sauce, vinegar, and mustard. Pour over chops. Cover; refrigerate at least 4 hours.
Drain chops; reserve liquid. Heat oil in medium skillet; brown chops over medium heat. Add ¼ cup marinade to chops. Cover; simmer chops 30 to 45 minutes, until tender.
Mix sugar, cornstarch, and remaining marinade in a small saucepan. Heat to a boil, stirring constantly. Simmer for 5 minutes more. Add pineapple chunks; heat through. Spoon over chops; serve.

lamb chops italian

Yield: 4 to 6 servings

1 tablespoon shortening
6 lean shoulder lamb chops
1½ cups water
1 8-ounce can tomato sauce
¼ cup catsup

1 tablespoon Worcestershire sauce
½ teaspoon oregano
1 clove garlic, crushed fine
1 teaspoon salt
½ teaspoon pepper

This dish combines skillet with oven, so preheat oven to 350°F.

Melt shortening in a large skillet; brown chops on both sides. Place chops in shallow baking pan.

Pour water into skillet, stirring to loosen particles on bottom of pan. Add remaining ingredients to liquid, stirring over low heat until blended, about 2 minutes. Pour this over chops. Cover the baking pan; bake chops 1 hour.

lamb chops italian

stuffed pork tenderloin

Yield: 6 servings

1 pork tenderloin
12 prunes, pitted
4 tablespoons butter
1 teaspoon salt

Dash of freshly ground
   black pepper
½ cup water

With a sharp knife cut a slit in the meat deep enough to insert the prunes. After prunes are inserted, close the opening with skewers, or wrap with twine.

Melt butter in large skillet and brown the meat on all sides. Sprinkle with salt and pepper. Add ½ cup water; cover, and cook slowly 2 hours or until meat is tender. Add more water if needed. Slice and serve.

Thicken juice in the pan slightly if gravy is desired.

stuffed pork tenderloin

51

quick-and-easy pork chops

Two ingredients make an easy dish, and, while this is cooking, you can be freshening up in the shower, throw a salad together, and still have a meal on your table in short order.

Yield: 4 to 6 servings

4 to 6 large pork chops
1 10½-ounce can condensed onion soup

In medium skillet lightly brown pork chops in their own fat. When both sides are browned, add onion soup to chops. Cover; reduce heat to simmer. Cook slowly 1 hour.

For company, add a spoonful of sour cream on top of each chop.

pork chops with apples

Yield: 4 servings

1 pound pork chops (cut from a roast)
Salt
Black pepper
2 tablespoons butter
2 onions
2 apples
Parsley

Salt the pork chops; spice them with pepper.

Heat butter in a deep skillet; brown the meat. Add enough water so that meat does not stick to skillet. Cover and cook on low heat at least 1 hour.

Peel onions; cut them into rings. Core and peel apples; cut them into eighths. Add onions and apples 10 minutes before end of cooking period. Cook until all ingredients are golden brown.

Remove chops; put them on a serving platter. Pour stock, onions, and apples over meat; garnish with parsley.

pork chops in white wine

pork chops in white wine

Yield: 4 servings

4 lean pork chops, about 1 inch thick	2 teaspoons flour
Salt and pepper to taste	½ cup chicken broth
1 teaspoon bacon drippings	½ cup dry white wine
	1 large onion, sliced

Season chops with salt and pepper. In medium skillet sear pork chops slowly on both sides in hot bacon fat. Remove chops from skillet.

Stirring constantly, blend flour into remaining fat in skillet. When very smooth, return chops to skillet with broth and wine. Spread sliced onion over chops. Cover skillet; simmer about 45 minutes.

Rice or mashed potatoes plus a salad complete the meal.

apricot veal birds

Yield: 4 to 6 servings

½ cup chopped dried apricots
¼ cup chopped celery
½ cup soft bread crumbs
1 teaspoon sugar
12 thin veal scallops
¼ cup oil
2 teaspoons salt
Dash of pepper
1 cup water

Combine apricots, celery, crumbs, and sugar in a bowl. This is your stuffing for the veal. Place 1 tablespoon stuffing on each veal slice. Roll up each slice and secure it with a wooden toothpick.

Heat oil in large skillet. Sauté veal birds until well-browned on all sides. Season meat with salt and pepper. Add water; cover skillet. Simmer for 30 minutes, until tender to the fork. Remove skewers before serving.

veal cutlets with zucchini

Good eating combines with good dietary habits here. This is also good for calorie-counters and those who watch their cholesterol.

Yield: 6 servings

6 veal cutlets
2 egg whites, slightly beaten
½ cup bread crumbs
4 tablespoons oil
2 cups canned tomatoes
1½ teaspoons salt
¼ teaspoon oregano
3 medium zucchini, sliced ½ inch thick

Dip cutlets first in egg whites, then in crumbs.

Brown cutlets in heated oil in large skillet. Pour off excess oil. Add tomatoes, salt, and oregano. Cover skillet; simmer for 30 minutes. Last, add zucchini slices; cook, covered, for 20 minutes more.

veal scallops in sour cream

Yield: 4 servings

4 veal scallops, no more than
   ½ inch thick
3 tablespoons butter
3 tablespoons vegetable oil
¼ cup finely chopped onion

1 cup sour cream
½ cup shredded Norwegian
   goat cheese
Salt to taste
Freshly ground pepper to taste

Pound scallops to ¼ inch thickness. Set aside.

Melt 1 tablespoon butter and 1 tablespoon oil in a large skillet. Add finely chopped onion; cook for 3 to 5 minutes. Do not brown the onion. Take onion from skillet and set aside.

Add remaining butter and oil to skillet; fry veal scallops over moderate heat until golden brown, about 5 minutes per side. Keep scallops warm in a low oven while you prepare the sauce.

Pour off most of fat left in skillet. Add onion and cook again 2 to 5 minutes. On low heat slowly stir in the sour cream and cheese. Continue stirring until sauce is smooth. Add seasonings to taste. Return veal to sauce. Baste meat and let it simmer for 2 minutes. Serve at once.

veal with artichoke hearts

Yield: 4 to 6 servings

2 cloves garlic
2 tablespoons oil
2 pounds veal round, pounded thin
   and cut in bite-size pieces
Salt and pepper to taste
2 cups canned tomatoes
½ cup sherry or dry white wine
¼ teaspoon oregano
2 10-ounce packages frozen artichoke hearts

Sauté garlic in oil in large skillet. Remove garlic.

Season veal generously with salt and pepper. Brown veal in oil. Add tomatoes, wine, and oregano, mixing well. Last, add artichoke hearts. Cover skillet; simmer for 1 hour. Meat should be tender when served.

Serve this veal with broad noodles and a tossed salad.

veal and noodles

Yield: 4 servings

1 tablespoon shortening or oil
1 pound ground veal
1 medium onion, chopped
1 green pepper, chopped
1 can tomato soup
1 cup water

1 cup noodles
2 tablespoons margarine
2 cups creamed corn
½ cup chopped ripe olives
1 cup grated cheese for garnish

Heat oil in medium skillet; brown together the veal, onion, and green pepper. Add soup, water, and noodles; simmer for 5 minutes. Add margarine, corn, and olives; cover. Simmer for 15 minutes or until noodles are tender.

Sprinkle cheese on top of individual servings. Complete the meal with your favorite salad and hot rolls.

meatballs special

The oval shape of these meatballs gives eye-appeal as well as good taste—that extra touch that pleases palates.

Yield: 6 or more servings

1 pound veal
1 pound pork
¼ cup flour
1 tablespoon salt
½ teaspoon white pepper
4 eggs

½ cup light cream
1 cup milk
1 medium onion, chopped
1 tablespoon butter or shortening
Extra shortening if needed

Grind veal and pork together several times. Put in a large bowl. With your electric beater at low speed, add flour, salt, and pepper. Add eggs one at a time, still at low speed. Add cream and milk.

In large skillet brown onion in 1 tablespoon butter just 5 minutes. Add this mixture to meat. Mix enough so that meat can be easily handled.

Shape meat into oval cakes; brown on both sides, adding extra shortening if needed. Cook over low heat 15 minutes. Because pork is included, these meatballs must be thoroughly cooked.

meatballs special

meat patties

Yield: 8 to 10 patties

½ pound boneless veal
½ pound boneless pork
1 medium onion, grated
3 tablespoons flour
1½ cups club soda

1 egg
1 teaspoon salt
¼ teaspoon pepper
6 tablespoons butter or
    vegetable oil

Have butcher grind meats together twice.

Grate onion; mix with meat. Add flour; mix well. An electric beater can be used. Gradually add club soda; beat until meat is light. Last, add beaten egg, salt, and pepper. Cover bowl; refrigerate at least 1 hour, so that meat can be handled easily.

Shape meat into 4-inch rectangles, 1 inch thick.

Melt butter in large skillet; add meat patties a few at a time. Cook each batch at least 6 to 8 minutes per side. Since pork is in the mixture, meat must be cooked all the way through. The finished patties will be brown on the outside, with no tinge of pink in the center.

curried chicken

Yield: 6 or more servings

2 small chickens, about 3 pounds each	**3 cups boiling water**
1 medium onion, chopped	**2 teaspoons salt**
⅓ cup margarine	**¼ cup flour**
1 light tablespoon curry powder	

Cut each chicken into pieces.

Brown chopped onion in margarine in large skillet. Remove onion; brown the chicken parts in same fat. Replace onion; add curry powder. Pour 3 cups boiling water over chicken; add salt. Simmer until chicken is tender, about 30 minutes.

Mix flour with ¼ cup chicken liquid; add to chicken. Stir until thick and smooth.

Serve chicken piping hot on a bed of rice.

curried chicken

chicken with currant jelly

Yield: 4 to 6 servings

1 2- to 3-pound frying chicken, cut
    into serving pieces
Flour seasoned with salt and pepper
2 tablespoons margarine
2 tablespoons oil
½ cup currant jelly

1 teaspoon grated lemon rind
1 tablespoon soy sauce
1 cup orange juice
1 large green pepper, cut into
    1-inch pieces
Orange slices for garnish

Coat chicken with seasoned flour—shake it in a brown paper bag.
Heat margarine and oil in a large skillet; brown the chicken pieces.
Coat each browned chicken piece with currant jelly; return to skillet.
Combine lemon rind, soy sauce, and orange juice; pour over jellied chicken.
Cover skillet; simmer for 30 to 40 minutes or until chicken is tender. Baste several times. Last, add green pepper; simmer for 5 minutes more.
Serve at once, garnished with orange slices.

chicken delight

The Chinese flavor to this dish is a delight.

Yield: 4 to 6 servings

1 2- to 3-pound frying chicken, cut
    into serving pieces
Flour seasoned with salt, pepper,
    and garlic salt
2 tablespoons margarine
2 tablespoons oil
1 small can mandarin oranges
    with juice

4 tablespoons lemon juice
½ cup orange juice
2 tablespoons honey
2 teaspoons soy sauce
½ teaspoon ginger

Put seasoned flour in a brown paper bag. Shake chicken pieces in the bag to coat with flour mixture.
Heat margarine and oil in skillet; brown the chicken pieces.
Drain mandarin oranges, reserving juice.
Mix mandarin juice with lemon juice, orange juice, honey, soy sauce, and ginger. Pour this sauce over chicken in skillet. Cover; allow to simmer for 30 minutes. When chicken is tender to the fork, add mandarin oranges; simmer just 5 minutes more.

Picture on next pages: chicken delight

fried chicken with cream gravy

fried chicken with cream gravy

Yield: 4 to 6 servings

> Salt, pepper, and garlic salt
> 1 cup flour
> 1 2½- to 3-pound frying chicken, cut into serving pieces
> Fat for deep frying

Mix seasonings with flour; coat each piece of chicken with this.

Heat fat in skillet; fry chicken, a few pieces at a time. Cook about 25 minutes per batch of chicken, so that pieces are crisp and crusty. Drain on paper towels; set on a warmed platter.

cream gravy

> 2 tablespoons cornstarch
> ¾ cup hot chicken broth
> ½ cup milk at room temperature
> 1 teaspoon salt
> ¼ teaspoon pepper

Pour off most of fat in skillet, leaving about 2 tablespoons.

Mix cornstarch with chicken broth. Add to hot fat, stirring constantly. Gradually add milk, salt, and pepper. When slightly thickened, gravy is ready.

Put gravy in gravy boat and serve with chicken.

62

mock fried chicken

Yield: 4 to 6 servings

    **1 2½- to 3-pound frying chicken,
       cut into serving pieces
    1 teaspoon salt
    ¼ teaspoon pepper
    2 large onions, sliced into rings
    ½ cup water**

Put chicken pieces skin-side-down into a large, heavy skillet. Sprinkle chicken with salt and pepper; put onion slices on top. Cover skillet; cook chicken over low heat 30 minutes.

Tilt lid of skillet slightly to allow liquid to evaporate as it continues to cook slowly another 20 minutes. Chicken will be tender and golden. Remove chicken to a heated platter.

Put onions back in open skillet with the water. Stir together for several minutes, until onions darken and absorb the liquid. Spoon this over chicken; serve.

mock fried chicken

honey-glazed chicken

honey-glazed chicken

Yield: 4 to 6 servings

1 2- to 3-pound chicken, cut into pieces	Fat for frying chicken
¼ cup flour	1 cup orange juice
1 teaspoon salt	1 tablespoon honey
¼ teaspoon pepper	4 tablespoons soy sauce
	1 clove garlic, peeled and halved

Dredge chicken in mixture of flour, salt, and pepper. Fry in medium skillet; set aside to keep warm. Remove all but 1 tablespoon of fat from skillet.

Mix orange juice with other ingredients in same skillet. Bring to a boil; let bubble gently until reduced to a glaze, about 20 minutes. Remove garlic pieces. Dip chicken into glaze, coating thoroughly, and serve.

chicken espagnol

This chicken starts in the skillet and ends in the oven—an easy dish to prepare ahead and pop into the oven 1 hour before dinner.

Yield: 4 to 6 servings

    2 tablespoons oil
    1 2- to 3-pound frying chicken, cut into serving pieces
    Salt and pepper
    1 large onion, minced fine
    1 green pepper, seeded and chopped into 1-inch pieces
    1 small garlic clove, minced fine
    4 cups tomatoes, canned or fresh, diced
    ½ cup white wine
    ½ teaspoon thyme
    2 bay leaves

Preheat oven to 350°F.

Heat oil in heavy skillet; brown all chicken pieces. Remove chicken to a casserole; season well with salt and pepper.

Using same oil in skillet, brown the onion, green pepper, and garlic. Add remaining ingredients; heat. Pour this over chicken; bake at 350°F for 1 hour. The chicken will be tender and tasty.

chicken hungarian

Yield: 4 to 6 servings

    1 2½- to 3-pound frying chicken,
        cut into pieces
    5 tablespoons butter or margarine
    1 medium onion, sliced in rings
    1 tablespoon paprika
    ½ teaspoon celery salt
    ½ teaspoon garlic salt
    ½ cup hot water
    1 tablespoon cornstarch
    2 tablespoons cold water
    ½ pint sour cream

Brown the chicken pieces in butter. Add onion, seasonings, and hot water. Cover; simmer until chicken is tender, 30 to 45 minutes. Remove chicken pieces; keep them warm.

Mix cornstarch and water to form a paste. Stir into liquid left in skillet. Allow to thicken slightly. Slowly stir in sour cream until all is piping hot. Return chicken to pan; serve.

easy chicken of the islands

Bring zip to the dieter's menu with this chicken—it adds no fat and a brisk, tangy flavor to any meal.

Yield: 4 to 6 servings

1 2- to 3-pound frying chicken, cut into serving pieces	**1 clove garlic, minced fine**
½ cup vinegar	**Dash of freshly ground black pepper**
½ cup soy sauce	

In the skillet you use to cook the chicken, put vinegar, soy sauce, garlic, and pepper. Add chicken; allow this to marinate together at least 30 minutes. After chicken has marinated, heat on top of stove until it comes to a boil. Then cover skillet, lower the heat, and allow to simmer about 40 minutes. The liquid will be absorbed into the chicken.

This may be served either hot or cold.

chicken in lemon–dill butter

This is rich, but so good.

Yield: 4 to 6 servings

¼ pound butter or margarine
2 tablespoons lemon juice
1 teaspoon salt
1 clove garlic, minced
Dash of pepper

½ teaspoon paprika
1 can sliced mushrooms, drained
1 tablespoon dillweed
1 2½- to 3-pound frying chicken,
    cut into serving pieces

Melt butter in a large skillet. Add all ingredients in order given; bring mixture to a boil. Add chicken; again bring to a boil, but do not actually boil. Cover skillet, lower the heat, and simmer for 30 minutes or until chicken is tender.

Remove chicken to a platter and serve with noodles or rice, over which you pour the remaining liquid.

chicken in lemon–dill butter

chicken and meatballs

Yield: 6 to 8 servings

1 cup chopped celery
2 medium onions, chopped
1 green pepper, chopped
2 tablespoons margarine
1 pound ground beef or veal
1 onion, minced

Salt and pepper to taste
1 frying chicken, cut into
   serving pieces
Salt, pepper, and garlic salt to taste
2 cups water

Sauté celery, 2 chopped onions, and green pepper in margarine in a large skillet. Set aside.

Mix ground meat with minced onion and seasonings to taste. Form into meatballs. Season chicken pieces liberally.

Place meatballs on vegetables in skillet. Place chicken on top of meatballs. Add enough water to cover meatballs only. The chicken will steam. Cover skillet; cook at least 1 hour. You may want to simmer this longer. When chicken is tender, the dish is done.

This can all be prepared in the morning and reheated at mealtime.

mustard fried chicken

This recipe gives a delicious, different taste to fried chicken.

Yield: 4 to 6 servings

2 or more tablespoons dry mustard
¼ cup water
1 2½- to 3-pound frying chicken,
   cut into serving pieces
Flour seasoned with salt and pepper
Fat or oil for frying
1 can condensed cream of celery soup
1 cup plus 2 tablespoons milk
1 can condensed tomato soup

Mix dry mustard with water to form a thick paste. Spread paste liberally over chicken pieces. Dredge chicken with flour.

Heat fat in large skillet; cook chicken on all sides until golden brown. Remove from skillet.

Reduce fat in skillet to about 3 tablespoons. Add celery soup, milk, and tomato soup to skillet; mix well. Replace chicken in this gravy; cover skillet. Simmer for 30 minutes, until chicken is tender.

chicken and shrimp

Yield: 4 to 6 servings

 4 ounces dried mushrooms
 1 cup water
 1 3-pound frying chicken, cut into serving pieces
 3 tablespoons flour
 3 teaspoons salt
 ½ teaspoon freshly ground black pepper
 4 tablespoons shortening
 ⅓ cup port wine
 ¼ cup chili sauce
 ½ teaspoon rosemary
 ½ pound tiny cooked shrimp

Soak mushrooms in water overnight.

Place chicken in paper bag with flour, salt, and pepper.

Heat shortening in skillet; brown the chicken pieces. Add wine, chili sauce, rosemary, and mushrooms plus their liquid. Cover; simmer until chicken is tender, about 1 hour. This can be done ahead.

When ready to serve, reheat chicken, and add the shrimp. When all is hot, the dish is ready.

groundnut stew

This is an African dish that goes well with rice or mashed yams.

Yield: 8 to 10 servings

 1 2- to 3-pound frying chicken,   1 cup chopped onions
  cut into small pieces   1 green pepper, chopped
 Salt and pepper to taste   2 large tomatoes, peeled and diced
 1 pound beef cubes, 1-inch size   1½ teaspoons cayenne
 2 tablespoons oil (peanut oil is good)   2 cups water
 1 teaspoon salt   1½ cups peanut butter

Season chicken with salt and pepper; set aside.

Brown the beef cubes in hot oil in large skillet. Add salt, ½ of the onions, ½ of the pepper and tomatoes, cayenne, and water. Simmer this gently 30 minutes.

Mix 1 cup cooking liquid with peanut butter to make a smooth paste. Add to skillet; cook for 15 minutes more. Add chicken pieces and remainder of vegetables. Simmer for 30 minutes more, until all is tender.

walnut chicken

Yield: 4 to 6 servings

¼ cup soy sauce
1 tablespoon dry sherry
½ teaspoon ground ginger
1 pound boneless chicken breasts,
    cut into 1-inch pieces
4 tablespoons vegetable oil
½ cup sliced green onions
1 clove garlic, cut in half
1 cup coarsely chopped walnuts

Make a marinade of the soy sauce, sherry, and ginger. Add chicken pieces; let stand for ½ hour.

Heat large skillet (wok can be used). Add 2 tablespoons oil. Sauté onions, garlic, and walnuts 2 to 3 minutes. Remove garlic halves. Set aside onion and walnut mixture in a bowl.

Heat remaining oil; add chicken pieces with the liquid. Stir this about 5 minutes, then add walnuts and onions; stir together 2 minutes more.

Spoon the chicken mixture over hot rice and enjoy it.

chicken with almonds

Yield: 4 to 6 servings

3 tablespoons butter or margarine
3 tablespoons flour
1 cup milk
1 cup chicken broth
1 teaspoon salt
½ teaspoon freshly ground black pepper
Leftover sliced chicken (diced can be used)
2 tablespoons sherry
½ cup slivered almonds

Melt butter in medium skillet; blend in flour. Gradually stir in milk and chicken broth. Continue stirring until liquid thickens. Add salt, pepper, and chicken; simmer until hot. Blend in sherry; last, sprinkle with almonds. Save a few to garnish with.

Serve over hot toast squares.

chicken cutlets

Yield: 6 servings

2 tablespoons flour
2 cups chicken stock
3 egg yolks
3 cups diced, cooked chicken
12 mushrooms, finely diced
Salt and pepper to taste
1 whole egg, beaten
Bread or cracker crumbs
1 cup or more of shortening for deep frying

Mix flour with ¼ cup chicken stock in a large skillet. Gradually add rest of heated stock. Stir until thickened. Add beaten egg yolks to sauce. Add chicken, mushrooms, and seasonings. Stir constantly while mixture cooks for 5 minutes. Cool, then chill mixture several hours, so it becomes stiff.

Shape mixture into cutlets. Dip each cutlet into beaten egg, then into crumbs. Chill battered mixture again.

Fry cutlets in deep fat until thoroughly browned; serve.

chicken cooked ahead

A cook who likes to think ahead may double or triple this recipe in a larger skillet and freeze enough for several meals with one-time cooking.

Yield: 2 cups diced chicken

2 whole chicken breasts, split
2½ cups chicken broth

Place chicken breasts and broth into a medium-size skillet. Bring broth to boiling point. Cover; reduce heat to simmer. Cook for 20 minutes, until chicken is tender. Allow to cool.

Dice chicken into cubes, put into a freezer container with the broth, and freeze.

When you are ready for chicken salad or any of the meals calling for diced chicken, all you have to do is thaw, drain, and use it.

chicken a la king

chicken a la king

Yield: 6 to 8 servings

  ½ **pound mushrooms, sliced**
  ½ **cup butter or shortening**
  ½ **cup flour**
  2 **cups chicken broth**
  2 **cups light cream**
  2 **egg yolks, beaten**
  3 **cups diced cooked chicken or turkey**
  ½ **cup pimiento, cut into strips**
  1 **teaspoon salt**
  ¼ **teaspoon pepper**

Sauté mushrooms in butter in medium-sized, heavy skillet.

Mix flour with chicken broth; add to skillet. Stir; add cream. Simmer this 5 minutes. Add beaten egg yolks, chicken, and pimiento. Stir until thoroughly hot, but do not let mixture boil. Add salt and pepper.

Spoon over toast or English muffins. Peas always seem to complement chicken a la king.

company chicken breasts

Yield: 4 to 6 servings

¼ cup flour
1 teaspoon salt
¼ teaspoon oregano
¼ teaspoon pepper
4 chicken breasts, cut in half
5 tablespoons butter or margarine
¾ cup white wine

1 tablespoon lemon juice
1 cup sliced fresh mushrooms
½ cup finely chopped onions
2 medium tomatoes, diced
1 teaspoon sugar
¼ cup water

Blend flour, salt, oregano, and pepper. Set aside 1 tablespoon of this mixture for later.

Dredge chicken pieces in flour mixture.

Melt 3 tablespoons butter in large skillet; brown the chicken.

Combine wine and lemon juice; pour over chicken. Cover skillet; simmer for 30 to 45 minutes, until chicken is tender.

Sauté mushrooms and onions in butter in small skillet. Onions should be transparent.

Remove chicken to a warm platter and keep it warm.

Add mushrooms, onions, tomatoes, and sugar to sauce in large skillet. Cook over low heat 5 minutes, until tomatoes are tender.

Blend reserved flour with water; add to sauce. Stir until sauce thickens slightly. Pour over the waiting chicken; serve.

breast of chicken and ham

This dish can be made ahead and reheated in a slow oven before serving.

Yield: 4 to 6 servings

3 whole raw chicken breasts,
    boned, skinned, and halved
¼ cup flour
1 teaspoon salt
¼ teaspoon white pepper

3 tablespoons olive oil
3 tablespoons butter or margarine
½ teaspoon dried sage
6 slices ham
½ cup dry white wine

Put chicken between 2 pieces of waxed paper and pound very thin. Dip in mixture of flour, salt, and pepper.

Heat oil and butter in large skillet. Sauté chicken breasts until browned on underside. Turn and sprinkle each breast with sage. Lay a slice of ham on top of each chicken piece. Cook on low heat 5 minutes. Add wine; simmer for 2 minutes more.

Serve chicken with pan juices poured over it.

chicken breasts in white wine

Yield: 4 to 6 servings

1½ tablespoons flour	4 tablespoons butter
½ teaspoon salt	½ pound mushrooms, thinly sliced
Dash of pepper	¼ cup chopped onion
4 chicken breasts, boned and halved	¼ cup chopped parsley
	1 cup white wine

Combine flour, salt, and pepper. Coat chicken in this mixture. Shake off excess flour; save it.

Melt 2 tablespoons butter in large skillet. Brown the chicken; remove it from skillet.

Add remaining butter to skillet; add mushrooms, onion, and parsley. Cook until onion is transparent. Remove from heat. Stir in remaining flour; blend in wine. When all is smooth, return to heat; bring liquid to a boil. Add chicken. Cook 30 minutes more, until chicken is tender.

Garnish with extra parsley.

chicken breasts in white wine

chow-mein chicken

The fixings for this take time to do, but the cooking goes quickly. Rice and/or noodles make a fine complement for this dish.

Yield: 4 to 6 servings

2 cups raw chicken breasts, thinly sliced or julienne
2 tablespoons oil
1 small onion, thinly sliced
1 cup finely diced celery
1 cup sliced water chestnuts
1 5-ounce can bamboo shoots (1 cup)

1 10-ounce package snow pea pods
2 cups chicken broth
2 tablespoons soy sauce
1 teaspoon sugar
2 tablespoons cornstarch
¼ cup cold water
1 teaspoon salt
Slivered almonds for garnish

In a large skillet sauté chicken in oil just 3 minutes, stirring. Add onion and celery; cook uncovered 5 minutes more. Add water chestnuts, bamboo shoots, pea pods, broth, and soy sauce. Cover; cook for 5 minutes.

Blend sugar, cornstarch, and cold water. Pour over chicken; stir until slightly thickened. Add salt. Serve, garnished with nuts if desired.

chicken livers with beer

The cook will like the ease of this dish—the family will like the taste.

Yield: 4 to 6 servings

¼ pound butter or margarine
1 medium onion, chopped fine
¼ teaspoon garlic powder
1½ pounds chicken livers
1 tablespoon flour
½ cup beer
3 cups cooked rice

Melt butter in medium skillet; cook onion until transparent. Add garlic powder and chicken livers; cook until livers are browned on all sides.

Mix flour with 1 tablespoon beer; add to livers. Stirring constantly, add rest of beer until sauce thickens and livers are done through, about 5 minutes.

Put hot cooked rice in center of platter and mound the chicken livers around it.

chicken livers with sage

Since this is Italian, have cooked spaghetti ready.

Yield: 4 to 6 servings

    1 pound chicken livers, halved
    1 teaspoon salt
    ¼ teaspoon pepper
    1 tablespoon dried sage
    4 tablespoons butter or margarine
    2 slices raw bacon, diced fine
    ¼ cup dry white wine

Season chicken livers with salt, pepper, and sage.

Heat butter and bacon together in medium skillet. Add chicken livers; cook for 5 minutes, until browned. Stir in the wine; allow to simmer 2 minutes more.

Spoon chicken livers and sauce over spaghetti. Add a salad, and the meal is complete.

chicken livers on toast

Chicken livers are sure to be a hit this way.

Yield: 4 servings

    1 can mushroom gravy
    2 tablespoons sherry
    ½ cup flour
    ½ teaspoon dried dillweed
    1 pound chicken livers
    1 egg, beaten
    4 or more tablespoons butter or margarine

Mix mushroom gravy and sherry in a saucepan; bring to a boil. Lower heat; simmer for 5 minutes.

Combine flour and dillweed for batter. Put each chicken liver first into beaten egg, then into flour. Be sure to coat all sides of livers well.

Melt butter in medium skillet. Add chicken livers; cook over moderate heat 10 minutes or until livers are golden brown.

Serve on toast squares with hot gravy.

turkey sukiyaki

Yield: 4 to 6 servings

3 tablespoons oil
1 cup diced green pepper
1 cup celery, sliced on the diagonal
1 cup green onions, diced with tops
2 cups cooked, diced turkey
¼ cup soy sauce

Heat oil in medium skillet; add vegetables. Cook, stirring, over medium heat 5 minutes or until vegetables are tender but not mushy. Add turkey and soy sauce; stir until mixed and heated through.

Serve over piping-hot rice.

turkey sukiyaki

twice-turkey treat

You will bless this quick-and-easy way to use leftover turkey after any holiday. Delicious served over rice, open hamburger rolls, or toast.

Yield: 4 to 6 servings

  3 cups cooked diced turkey
  ½ pound mushrooms, sliced
  ½ cup chopped onion
  1 tablespoon oil or margarine
  3 tablespoons cornstarch
  1 cup chicken stock
  ½ teaspoon salt
  1½ teaspoons curry powder
  1 cup finely chopped apple
  ¼ cup chopped parsley
  ¾ cup skim milk

In medium skillet gently sauté turkey, mushrooms, and onion in oil until onion is transparent.

Mix cornstarch with chicken stock; add to skillet. Add salt, curry powder, chopped apple, and parsley. Add skim milk last. (If diet is no problem, use whole milk or cream.) Stir as you simmer for 3 minutes. The apples will be crisp and tender.

from the sea

butterfish in sour cream

Yield: 4 to 6 servings

2 pounds butterfish
Salt and pepper to taste
½ teaspoon salt
¾ cup flour
1 egg, beaten
½ cup milk

1 tablespoon melted butter or margarine
Fat for deep frying
1 cup sour cream
1 tablespoon chopped parsley
1 tablespoon minced green onion
1 tablespoon lemon juice

Season fish with salt and pepper.

In a bowl mix ½ teaspoon salt, flour, egg, milk, and melted butter to form a batter. Dip fish in this to coat it thoroughly.

In large skillet fry fish in hot, deep fat until golden brown all over. Drain fish and set on hot platter.

In a saucepan combine sour cream, parsley, onion, and lemon juice until just hot. Serve over the fried fish.

fisherman's crab meat

This entree goes together so fast it's hard to believe it's as good as it is.

Yield: 4 to 6 servings

½ cup vinegar
6 tablespoons melted butter
1 tablespoon chopped chives

2 teaspoons Worcestershire sauce
1 pound fresh lump crab meat

Heat vinegar, butter, chives, and Worcestershire sauce in medium skillet. Add crab meat; simmer until hot, stirring gently to blend flavors.

clam sauce supreme

Yield: 4 to 6 servings

> 2 tablespoons butter or margarine
> 1 tablespoon flour
> 1 teaspoon garlic salt
> 2 8-ounce cans minced clams with liquid
> 1 teaspoon parsley
> 1 teaspoon salt
> ½ teaspoon pepper
> Cooked thin spaghetti

In medium skillet melt butter on low heat. Stir in flour and garlic salt, using a wire whisk. Add juice from canned clams; continue to stir. Add seasonings and, last, the clams. Simmer this 10 minutes. Pour over cooked thin spaghetti.

clam cakes

Yield: 4 servings

> 3 medium potatoes, cooked and mashed
> 1 8-ounce can minced clams
> 1 medium onion, chopped
> 1 teaspoon chopped parsley
> 1 egg, beaten
> ½ cup flour
> 1 teaspoon salt
> Dash of pepper
> Oil for deep frying

To the dry mashed potatoes add clams with their juice, onion, and parsley. Mix together, then add egg, flour, and seasonings. This will be a fairly liquid mixture.

Heat oil for deep frying in skillet. If preferred, use half liquid shortening and half butter or margarine. Drop potato and clam mixture by spoonfuls into hot fat. Fry until crisp and brown on all sides. Drain on paper towels.

Serve with your favorite slaw.

coddies

coddies

Coddies are popular served on saltine crackers with plenty of mustard.

Yield: 4 to 6 servings

3 medium potatoes, cooked and mashed	1 teaspoon salt
¼ pound butter or margarine	¼ teaspoon pepper
3 eggs, beaten	1 tablespoon chopped parsley
1 medium onion, chopped fine	3 15-ounce cans codfish
	Fat for deep frying

Mash potatoes smooth; add butter while potatoes are still hot. Add beaten eggs, onion, salt, pepper, parsley, and codfish. Mix well; let stand at least 1 hour.

Shape coddies into 2-inch cakes.

Heat fat in medium-size skillet. Fry coddies until brown and crisp. Drain on paper towels.

soft-shelled crabs

Yield: 4 to 6 servings

> 4 tablespoons butter or margarine
> 2 tablespoons lemon juice
> 6 to 8 soft-shelled crabs, cleaned
> 1 tablespoon cornstarch or flour
> ¼ cup water

Heat butter and lemon juice in medium skillet. On medium heat, cook crabs until browned, 5 minutes per side. Remove crabs to a heated platter.

Mix cornstarch and water. Add to pan juices; stir until slightly thickened. Pour sauce over crabs. Serve at once.

crab bisque

Yield: 4 to 6 servings

> 1 medium onion, diced
> ½ green pepper, diced
> 2 tablespoons butter or margarine
> ¼ pound mushrooms, sliced
> 2 tomatoes, diced
> 1 pound crab meat
> 1 teaspoon salt
> Dash of cayenne
> 1½ cups cream
> 1 tablespoon minced parsley

In medium skillet sauté onion and green pepper in melted butter until onion is transparent. Add mushrooms; cook for 3 minutes more. Stir in tomatoes; cook again 3 minutes. Add remaining ingredients; heat mixture to a boil, but do not boil.

Add more parsley for garnish if desired. Serve over rice.

crab cakes

crab cakes

Yield: 4 to 6 servings

> 1 pound crab meat
> 1 egg yolk
> 1½ teaspoons salt
> Healthy dash of black pepper
> 1 teaspoon dry mustard
> 2 teaspoons Worcestershire sauce
> 1 tablespoon mayonnaise
> 1 tablespoon chopped parsley
> ½ teaspoon paprika
> 1 tablespoon melted butter
> Bread crumbs for coating cakes
> Liquid shortening for frying

Lightly toss crab meat and all ingredients (except bread crumbs) in order listed. When well-blended, shape into cakes. Roll each cake in bread crumbs until coated on all sides.

Heat shortening in skillet. Fry crab cakes quickly in hot fat until golden brown.

fish cakes

Yield: 4 to 6 servings

1 egg
1 tablespoon lemon juice
1 onion, minced fine
2 tablespoons prepared mustard
½ teaspoon salt
¼ teaspoon pepper

1 teaspoon parsley flakes
1 pound cooked fish, boned
    and flaked
¼ cup corn-flake crumbs (at least)
Fat for deep frying

Mix egg, lemon juice, onion, and seasonings in a bowl. Toss with flaked fish. Add enough corn-flake crumbs to allow you to shape fish cakes easily. Roll each cake in extra crumbs to coat the outside.

Heat fat in medium skillet; fry cakes until crisp and brown on the outside. Drain on paper towels, then place on a heated platter.

fish cakes

fish steak brazilian

"Instant coffee with fish?" you say. Try it. It's good.

Yield: 4 to 6 servings

2 pounds halibut steak or fish steak of your choice
1 tablespoon instant coffee
2 tablespoons lemon juice
4 tablespoons melted margarine or oil
1 teaspoon salt
1 teaspoon onion salt
Chopped parsley for garnish

Place fish steaks in shallow dish.

Dissolve instant coffee in lemon juice. Add oil, salt, and onion salt to this. Pour over fish to marinate it. Let stand 30 minutes, turning once so both sides of steak absorb flavor.

Heat 4 tablespoons of marinade in skillet. When hot but not bubbling, add fish steaks; cook for 5 to 7 minutes per side. When both sides are cooked tender, add remaining marinade; simmer for 2 minutes more. Garnish with parsley; serve.

flounder with shrimp

Yield: 4 servings

Salt
4 fillets of flounder
Flour
2 eggs
2 tablespoons water
Bread crumbs
8 tablespoons butter
½ pound small cooked shrimp
Lemon wedges

Salt fillets lightly; dip in flour, being sure to shake off excess.

Beat eggs together with water.

Put bread crumbs on wax paper.

Batter fish by dipping each fillet first in egg mixture, then in bread crumbs, coating each side thoroughly. Set aside battered fish at least 10 minutes.

Heat 4 tablespoons butter in a medium skillet. Sauté fillets 3 to 4 minutes. Keep them warm while preparing shrimp.

Melt 4 tablespoons butter in a separate skillet. Toss shrimp in butter so that each shrimp becomes coated with butter. Place shrimp down the center of each fillet; pour browned butter over fillets.

Garnish with lemon wedges; serve.

haddock potato cakes

These are filling and are sure to be favorites for you.

Yield: 4 to 6 servings

4 medium potatoes, cooked and mashed
1 pound haddock fillets, cooked and flaked
1 egg, beaten
2 tablespoons minced onion
1 teaspoon seafood seasoning
¼ cup flour
Fat for deep frying

Mix together potatoes, fish, egg, onion, and seafood seasoning. Form into flat cakes; batter each one in flour.

Heat fat in skillet; drop cakes into fat. When fish cakes are browned on both sides, drain on paper towels.

sherry delight

Spices and wine blend here to make a sauce supreme. If you prefer, substitute sherry for the last ½ cup of water.

Yield: 4 servings

1½ pounds haddock fish fillets	Water
¼ cup flour	½ teaspoon freshly ground black pepper
¼ cup oil	¼ cup chives or ends of spring onions
½ teaspoon sugar	1 tablespoon parsley
½ teaspoon ginger	2 medium-size tomatoes, chopped
¼ teaspoon garlic powder	1 teaspoon cornstarch
1 tablespoon soy sauce	Salt to taste
1 tablespoon sherry	½ cup water or sherry

Coat fillets with flour.

Heat oil in skillet; brown fish on both sides.

Combine sugar, ginger, garlic, soy sauce, sherry, and water to make 1 cup. Pour over fish. Cover skillet; simmer for 10 minutes. Add black pepper, chives, parsley, and tomatoes. Cook uncovered for 5 minutes.

Mix together cornstarch, salt, and ½ cup water or sherry. Blend well; add to fish. Simmer uncovered 5 minutes more. Sauce will thicken slightly and smell heavenly.

oysters baltimore

Yield: 4 to 6 servings

4 slices bacon
18 oysters
3 tablespoons chili sauce
1 tablespoon Worcestershire sauce
6 tablespoons heavy cream
½ teaspoon tarragon
2 tablespoons lemon juice
1 teaspoon salt
¼ teaspoon pepper

In medium-size skillet fry bacon until crisp. Set bacon aside to drain, then crumble into bits for garnish.

Pour off all but 1 tablespoon fat from skillet. Add oysters with their liquid. Cook uncovered over medium heat until most of pan juices are absorbed.

Mix remaining ingredients; add to oysters. Simmer no more than 5 minutes to blend all flavors. Add extra seasonings if desired.

These oysters are delicious served over hot buttered toast. Garnish with crumbled bacon.

salmon croquettes

Yield: About 12 croquettes

2 cups canned salmon, drained   **1 tablespoon chopped parsley**
2 cups mashed potatoes   **1 teaspoon lemon juice**
1½ teaspoons salt   **Flour**
⅛ teaspoon pepper   **Seasoned bread crumbs**
1 beaten egg   **Fat for deep frying**

Mix together in a large bowl the salmon, potatoes, salt, pepper, beaten egg, parsley, and lemon juice. This should be a fairly dry mixture that can be easily shaped into croquettes. (Refrigerate it for an hour before shaping.)

When croquettes are ready to be fried, roll them first in flour, then in seasoned bread crumbs.

Heat fat in skillet. Put in a few croquettes, so they will have room to brown evenly on all sides. Cook about 3 minutes each. Drain on paper towels; keep them warm on a heated platter until finished cooking all.

salmon steaks with dill

Yield: 4 servings

    2 tablespoons margarine
    2 tablespoons oil
    4 salmon steaks
    4 tablespoons lemon juice
    1 tablespoon dillweed
    1 teaspoon salt
    Dash of freshly ground black pepper
    Chopped parsley for garnish

Heat margarine and oil in skillet. Put salmon steaks into hot fat.

Mix lemon juice, dillweed, salt, and pepper. Sprinkle half the liquid over steaks. Cover skillet; cook for 5 minutes. Turn salmon steaks; sprinkle with remaining liquid. Cover again; cook for 5 minutes more. Remove steaks to warm platter.

Add parsley to juices in skillet; pour over steaks. Serve at once.

dill scallops in lemon butter

Yield: 4 to 6 servings

    1½ pounds scallops
    ½ cup dry bread crumbs
    8 tablespoons butter or margarine
    ¼ teaspoon salt
    Dash of pepper
    Dash of paprika
    1 tablespoon chopped parsley
    2 teaspoons dillweed
    3 tablespoons lemon juice

Batter scallops in bread crumbs until well-coated.

Melt 4 tablespoons butter in skillet; add salt, pepper, and paprika. Sauté scallops slowly until evenly browned, about 8 minutes. Remove scallops to a heated platter. Add remaining butter to skillet with parsley, dill, and lemon juice. Stir until hot, then pour over scallops. Serve at once.

fried scallops with dill

Yield: 4 to 6 servings

1 pound scallops	**Seasoned bread crumbs**
1 egg with 2 tablespoons water	**Deep fat for frying**
2 teaspoons dillweed	

Wash scallops quickly; dry them between paper towels.

Beat the egg, water, and dillweed together.

Dip each scallop in the egg mixture, then in bread crumbs. Repeat this process once, then let scallops stand for 30 minutes.

Heat fat for frying in a medium-size skillet. Fry each scallop for 3 or 4 minutes. Drain and serve.

florida fish fillets

Yield: 4 servings

florida fish fillets

¼ cup flour
1 teaspoon dillweed
1 teaspoon salt
4 small fish fillets, skinned
4 tablespoons butter or margarine
Grapefruit and/or orange rings

Mix flour and seasonings; use to batter fillets.

Heat butter in medium skillet; sauté fillets until golden brown on both sides. Remove from skillet to a hot platter.

Put grapefruit slices or orange rings on top of each fillet. Pour pan gravy over all. Serve at once.

fish fillets india

Curry and chutney from the Far East make a treat of your favorite fish. Rice completes the meal.

Yield: 4 servings

½ cup flour
2 teaspoons curry powder
¼ teaspoon salt
1 pound fresh or frozen fillets (your choice of favorite fish)

½ cup margarine
½ cup chopped blanched almonds
Chutney

Mix flour, curry powder, and salt well. Thoroughly coat each piece of fish with this mixture.

Heat margarine in a large skillet. Brown the fish over moderate heat, about 4 minutes per side. When fish flakes easily, it is done through. Remove fillets; put them on a heated serving dish.

Add almonds to shortening left in skillet; stir until nuts are browned. Pour over fish.

Serve the chutney as a relish.

fillets in creole sauce

fillets in creole sauce

Delicious, fast, and easy.

Yield: 4 to 6 servings

1 medium onion, chopped	½ teaspoon curry powder
½ cup celery, chopped	Dash of freshly ground black pepper
1 tablespoon butter or margarine	1 cup chopped green pepper
1 8-ounce can tomato sauce	2 pounds frozen fish fillets of
½ teaspoon salt	your choice

Sauté onion and celery in butter in a large skillet. Add rest of ingredients except fish. Simmer mixture while you cut fish blocks in thirds, giving you 6 pieces. Put fish blocks in skillet side by side. Do not pile them on each other. Bring to a boil, then reduce to a simmer. Cook about 15 minutes or until fish flakes easily.

butterfly shrimp

Yield: 4 to 6 servings

> 1½ pounds large shrimp, cleaned
>   and deveined, leaving tails on
> ¾ cup flour
> 1 teaspoon baking powder
> ½ teaspoon salt
> ¾ cup milk
> 1 egg, beaten
> Fat for frying

Cut almost through shrimp lengthwise; spread out to form the butterfly. This is a trick of the knife that gets easier as you go along.

Mix flour, baking powder, and salt with milk and beaten egg. Stir until very smooth.

Heat fat in skillet.

Batter each shrimp; put into hot fat. Fry until golden brown, about 7 minutes. Drain cooked shrimp on paper towels.

Serve as is or with your favorite sauce.

skillet shrimp gumbo

Prepare the shrimp and rice ahead, then this is a fast put-together for any time of year.

Yield: 6 servings

> ⅓ cup oil
> 2 cups sliced fresh okra or
>   1 package frozen okra, sliced
> 1 pound shrimp, peeled
>   and deveined
> ½ cup chopped green onions
>   and tops
> 3 cloves garlic, minced fine
>
> 1½ teaspoons salt
> ½ teaspoon freshly ground
>   pepper
> 2 cups water
> 1 cup canned tomatoes, drained
> 2 whole bay leaves
> 6 drops Tabasco sauce
> 1½ cups cooked rice

Heat oil in a large skillet. Cook okra 10 minutes, stirring occasionally. Add shrimp, onions, garlic, salt, and pepper. Simmer for 5 minutes. Add water, tomatoes, and bay leaves. Cover; simmer for 20 minutes. Remove bay leaves; stir in Tabasco.

Place a liberal scoop of rice in each soup bowl. Fill to the top with gumbo. Serve.

shrimp marinara

This marinara is equally good using fish, crab, or lobster as its base.

Yield: 4 to 6 servings

    2 pounds shrimp, shelled and deveined
    2 tablespoons olive oil
    1 medium onion, chopped
    2 garlic cloves, crushed fine
    1 teaspoon salt
    1 tablespoon soft bread crumbs
    1 small tomato, chopped
    ¼ teaspoon oregano
    ½ cup dry sherry wine
    ½ cup water

In large skillet sauté shrimp in oil on moderate heat. When lightly browned, add onion, garlic, salt, and bread crumbs. Cook for 2 minutes, stirring to blend. Add tomato and oregano. Simmer for 3 minutes. Last, add sherry and water; simmer for 3 minutes more. Serve hot.

sweet-and-sour shrimp

Yield: 4 to 6 servings

    ¼ cup brown sugar
    1½ tablespoons cornstarch
    ½ teaspoon salt
    ¼ cup vinegar
    1 tablespoon soy sauce
    ½ teaspoon ground ginger
    1 20-ounce can pineapple chunks
    1 green pepper, diced
    1 medium onion, sliced in rings
    1 pound shrimp, cleaned, shelled, and cooked
    4 cups hot cooked rice

Into large skillet put sugar, cornstarch, salt, vinegar, soy sauce, ginger, and liquid from canned pineapple. Stir as you cook liquid until it thickens. Add pineapple, pepper, and onion; cook for 3 minutes. Last, add cooked shrimp. Continue to stir until all is hot.

Serve on a bed of rice and enjoy.

shrimp in wine sauce

shrimp in wine sauce

Serve this over hot rice and mop up the sauce with some good French bread. You won't want to leave a drop.

Yield: 4 to 6 servings

2 tablespoons butter or margarine
1 pound cooked shrimp, shelled
    and deveined
1 tablespoon cornstarch

½ teaspoon seafood seasoning
¼ cup dry sherry
2 tablespoons water

Melt butter in medium skillet; sauté shrimp 2 minutes.

Mix cornstarch and seafood seasoning with sherry and water until very smooth. Add to shrimp; stir until sauce is thickened, about 5 minutes.

seafood scampi

Yield: 6 to 8 servings

12 tablespoons margarine
6 cloves garlic, crushed
1 teaspoon salt
1½ pounds shrimp, cleaned
and deveined

1½ pounds raw fish, your choice,
cut in chunks
4 spring onions, chopped
½ cup chopped parsley

Melt margarine in large skillet. Add garlic and salt, then add seafood; cook for 5 minutes, stirring constantly. When shrimp is pink and fish flakes tender, add spring onions and parsley. Cook for 3 minutes more.

Add a Chinese touch to the scampi by serving over Chinese noodles.

seafood linguine

Yield: 4 to 6 servings

¼ pound butter or margarine
2 cans minced clams, drained
1 clove garlic, minced fine
1 teaspoon salt
¼ teaspoon pepper
½ pound shrimp, cooked and deveined
2 teaspoons lemon juice
1 pound linguine, cooked

Melt butter in medium skillet. Add all ingredients (except linguine) in order given. Cook on low heat 15 minutes, stirring occasionally. Pour over linguine; serve.

seafood newburg

seafood newburg

Yield: 6 to 8 servings

**4 tablespoons butter
      or margarine**
**4 cups fresh or frozen
      uncooked seafood
      (lobster, shrimp, crab meat,
      or fish fillets, all in
      1-inch pieces)**
3 tablespoons lemon juice
1 tablespoon flour
1 teaspoon salt
½ teaspoon paprika
⅛ teaspoon cayenne pepper
2 cups light cream
3 egg yolks
2 tablespoons sherry
6 cups hot cooked rice
Parsley for garnish

Melt butter in large skillet. Sauté seafood about 5 minutes, stirring constantly. Sprinkle with lemon juice.

Mix flour, salt, paprika, and pepper; add to seafood. Remove from heat. Gradually stir in 1½ cups of cream. Return to heat until sauce comes to simmer.

Combine egg yolks with remaining ½ cup cream; blend ¼ cup hot liquid mixture with this. Return this to skillet; stir until slightly thickened. Add sherry last, and liberally if you prefer.

Serve over rice, garnished with parsley.

fried smelts

fried smelts

Smelts are special because they are small fish with a very sweet flavor.

Yield: 4 to 6 servings

2 pounds smelts, heads off, cleaned, and washed
2 eggs, beaten
2 tablespoons milk
1 teaspoon salt
¼ teaspoon pepper
½ cup flour
½ cup dried bread crumbs or cracker crumbs
Fat for frying

Drain smelts as dry as possible on paper towels.
Mix eggs, milk, and seasonings in a bowl.
Mix flour and bread crumbs together on a large piece of wax paper. Dip each smelt in the liquid and then in crumbs.
Heat fat in skillet. Add smelts, cooking them until crisp and brown. If deep fat is used, cook about 10 minutes. If you prefer less fat, cook about 5 minutes per side. Drain on paper towels and serve.

fillets of sole

Yield: 4 to 6 servings

   2 pounds fish fillets
   ½ cup or more milk
   ¼ cup or more flour
   1 teaspoon salt
   3 teaspoons dillweed
   8 tablespoons butter
   Blanched toasted almonds for garnish
   Lemon slices

Dip the fillets in milk, then dust them with flour. Sprinkle them generously with salt and dillweed.

Melt 4 tablespoons butter in a medium-size skillet. Sauté the fillets, turning them once. When done, remove to a serving platter.

Add the remaining butter to the skillet; allow it to brown. Pour this over the fillets; sprinkle the almonds on top. Use lemon slices for garnish around the platter.

fisherman's trout

Yield: 4 servings

   4 (approximately 8-inch) brook trout
   Flour seasoned with lemon pepper
   ¼ cup butter or margarine
   3 tablespoons more butter or margarine
   Lemon wedges

Clean and wash the trout, cutting off the fins. Leave head and tail on or not, as desired.

Dip the cleaned trout in seasoned flour.

Melt ¼ cup of butter in a large skillet; sauté the trout until they are tender and browned on both sides. Remove to a hot platter.

Add the remaining 3 tablespoons of butter to the skillet; allow it to brown. Pour this over the fish. Serve the fish with lemon wedges.

mandarin tuna

The Chinese flavor changes tuna fish into a treat. Serve the tuna over hot rice, of course.

Yield: 4 to 6 servings

 4 tablespoons oil
 1 large clove garlic, minced
 1 cup celery strips, cut on the diagonal
 1 large onion, diced coarsely
 1 green pepper, cut in strips
 2 tablespoons cornstarch
 1 cup water
 1 tablespoon soy sauce
 1 teaspoon salt
 1 13-ounce can tuna, drained and flaked
 ½ cup sautéed almonds (optional)

Heat oil in medium skillet; add garlic, celery, onion, and green pepper. Stir until slightly tender but still crisp.

Blend cornstarch with 2 tablespoons water.

Add remaining water and soy sauce to skillet. Stir in cornstarch mixture. Add salt and tuna, continuing to stir gently until sauce thickens slightly.

Serve with rice garnished with almonds.

vegetables

winter bean sprouts

Dress up canned vegetables in winter with a fresh-cooked taste. Bean sprouts are easy on calory counters and taste good, too.

Yield: 4 to 6 servings

1 tablespoon margarine
2 medium onions, sliced in rings
2 cups bean sprouts (1 1-pound can, drained)
½ teaspoon salt
1 teaspoon soy sauce (optional)
1 teaspoon lemon juice

Melt margarine in medium skillet and lightly tan onions. Add rest of ingredients, stirring to blend flavors. Cover skillet; simmer for 1 minute. Serve at once.

dressed-up green beans

Yield: 4 to 6 servings

1 cup chicken stock
2 tablespoons chopped onions
¼ cup chopped green pepper
½ teaspoon dillseed
2 9-ounce packages frozen cut green beans

Heat chicken stock in medium skillet. Add onions, green pepper, and dillseed. Cook for 3 minutes to release flavors, then add green beans. Cover; simmer for 10 minutes or just until beans are tender.

vegetables

winter bean sprouts

Dress up canned vegetables in winter with a fresh-cooked taste. Bean sprouts are easy on calory counters and taste good, too.

Yield: 4 to 6 servings

1 tablespoon margarine
2 medium onions, sliced in rings
2 cups bean sprouts (1 1-pound can, drained)
½ teaspoon salt
1 teaspoon soy sauce (optional)
1 teaspoon lemon juice

Melt margarine in medium skillet and lightly tan onions. Add rest of ingredients, stirring to blend flavors. Cover skillet; simmer for 1 minute. Serve at once.

dressed-up green beans

Yield: 4 to 6 servings

1 cup chicken stock
2 tablespoons chopped onions
¼ cup chopped green pepper
½ teaspoon dillseed
2 9-ounce packages frozen cut green beans

Heat chicken stock in medium skillet. Add onions, green pepper, and dillseed. Cook for 3 minutes to release flavors, then add green beans. Cover; simmer for 10 minutes or just until beans are tender.

mandarin tuna

The Chinese flavor changes tuna fish into a treat. Serve the tuna over hot rice, of course.

Yield: 4 to 6 servings

> 4 tablespoons oil
> 1 large clove garlic, minced
> 1 cup celery strips, cut on the diagonal
> 1 large onion, diced coarsely
> 1 green pepper, cut in strips
> 2 tablespoons cornstarch
> 1 cup water
> 1 tablespoon soy sauce
> 1 teaspoon salt
> 1 13-ounce can tuna, drained and flaked
> ½ cup sautéed almonds (optional)

Heat oil in medium skillet; add garlic, celery, onion, and green pepper. Stir until slightly tender but still crisp.

Blend cornstarch with 2 tablespoons water.

Add remaining water and soy sauce to skillet. Stir in cornstarch mixture. Add salt and tuna, continuing to stir gently until sauce thickens slightly.

Serve with rice garnished with almonds.

red cabbage

Yield: 6 to 8 servings

    1 large head red cabbage
    2 tablespoons bacon fat or oil
    ½ cup red wine
    3 tablespoons red currant jelly
    1 teaspoon salt
    Dash of pepper
    1 tablespoon sugar
    Pinch of powdered cloves

Wash, shred, and drain cabbage.

Heat bacon fat or oil in large skillet. Add cabbage; heat for 5 minutes. Heating will wilt cabbage enough that it will all fit into pan. Add wine, jelly, salt, pepper, sugar, and cloves. Mix very well; continue to stir for a few minutes, until all flavors are absorbed. Cover; cook over low heat 25 minutes. Serve hot.

red cabbage and apples

Yield: 6 to 8 servings

    1 medium head red cabbage
    4 tablespoons butter or margarine
    2 medium onions, chopped
    ½ teaspoon nutmeg
    2 teaspoons salt
    ½ teaspoon ground black pepper
    2 cups water
    2 tablespoons cider vinegar
    4 firm apples, peeled, cored, and sliced
    3 tablespoons fresh lemon juice

Quarter the cabbage, remove hard core, and shred it.

Melt butter in large skillet. Add onions, nutmeg, salt, and pepper. Cook until onions are just golden. Add water and vinegar; gradually add cabbage, stirring as you do. Cover; cook over medium heat for 30 minutes.

Add sliced apples; continue cooking, covered, for no more than 30 minutes. Add extra water if needed. Stir in lemon juice just before serving.

red cabbage

red cabbage and apples

sautéed grated carrots

When prepared this way, carrots have fresh texture and flavor and are pretty enough to serve for a party.

Yield: 4 to 6 servings

4 tablespoons melted margarine
3 to 4 cups grated carrots
1 tablespoon lemon juice
1 tablespoon honey or thick corn syrup
½ teaspoon salt
1 tablespoon chopped chives
2 tablespoons white wine (optional)

To the melted margarine add grated carrots and rest of ingredients in order given. Stir several times to mix thoroughly. Simmer mixture in covered skillet 10 to 15 minutes.

carrots and grapes supreme

Don't waste this on general family eating unless you feed gourmets. It's definitely party fare.

Yield: 4 to 6 servings

4 cups Belgium carrots, drained
½ pound white grapes, rinsed
¼ pound margarine
½ cup cointreau

After carrots are drained and grapes rinsed, place them between paper towels until very dry.
Melt margarine in medium-size skillet. Add cointreau, carrots, and grapes. Simmer together 10 minutes.
Serve with a proud flourish.

dill fried cauliflower

Yield: 4 to 6 servings

    1 head cauliflower
    ½ cup bread crumbs mixed
      with 1 teaspoon salt
    1 teaspoon dillweed
    ¼ teaspoon pepper
    2 eggs, beaten
    4 tablespoons oil or chicken fat

Cook cauliflower in salted water just 10 minutes. Drain, cool, and separate into florets.

Dip each piece into seasoned bread crumbs. Then dip in beaten egg and return to crumb mixture.

Heat fat in medium skillet; cook florets until golden brown. Drain on paper towels; sprinkle with more salt and pepper if desired.

cauliflower sautéed

This makes a party dish out of a common vegetable. The cauliflower should be steamed a day ahead.

Yield: 4 to 6 servings

    2 tablespoons butter or margarine
    2 tablespoons salad oil
    1 teaspoon garlic salt
    1 head cauliflower, broken into florets
    1 teaspoon salt
    ½ teaspoon nutmeg
    Chopped chives for garnish

Melt the butter and salad oil in a medium-size skillet. Mix in the garlic salt; sauté the florets for 3 minutes, stirring gently. Season with salt and nutmeg.

Put the cauliflower into a serving bowl; garnish it with chopped chives.

glazed carrots

Yield: 4 to 6 servings

10 to 12 small young carrots,
    washed and trimmed
2 tablespoons margarine

1 tablespoon brown sugar
2 tablespoons honey
2 tablespoons fresh mint

Cook prepared carrots in small amount of boiling salted water 10 minutes. When tender, drain and set aside.

Melt margarine in medium skillet. Add sugar and honey; when blended, put in carrots. Cook 3 or 4 minutes over low heat, stirring so that each carrot is glazed. Sprinkle with fresh mint; serve.

(Parsley is a substitute for the fresh mint, if preferred.)

carrots and raisins

Yield: 4 to 6 servings

2 tablespoons butter or margarine
1½ pounds young carrots, scraped
    and cut into ¼-inch slices
    (try a diagonal slice—it's pretty)

⅓ cup water or dry white wine
½ teaspoon ground nutmeg
⅔ cup white raisins
3 teaspoons light brown sugar

Melt butter in medium skillet. Add carrots, water, and nutmeg. Cover; cook over low heat 15 minutes. Stir in raisins and sugar; cook for 5 minutes more or until raisins are plump and carrots are glazed.

french-fried fennel

Yield: 4 servings

1 large head fennel
½ cup flour
1 egg, beaten

½ cup milk
Salt and pepper to taste
Fat for deep frying

Slice white part of fennel into ¼-inch rings. Wash and pat dry. Save some green leaves to garnish the platter.

Mix flour, egg, milk, and seasonings in a bowl. This will be a smooth batter.

Heat oil in medium skillet. While oil is heating, dip pieces of fennel into batter. Then deep fry them just 2 minutes, until crusty and brown. After draining, put them on a heated platter and garnish with green fennel leaves.

Picture on opposite page: glazed carrots

corn fritters

Yield: 4 to 6 servings

1 1-pound can whole-kernel corn, drained
1 egg
½ teaspoon salt
¼ cup milk
1 cup flour
2 teaspoons baking powder
2 teaspoons melted butter or
margarine
½ teaspoon sugar
Deep fat for frying

While allowing corn to drain, mix egg, salt, milk, flour, baking powder, melted butter, and sugar. Stir with a wooden spoon—you don't need a mixer for this. Add drained corn. After corn is mixed in allow to sit for 5 minutes.

Drop mixture by teaspoonfuls into hot fat. Cook until puffy and golden brown, drain on paper, and transfer to a warmed platter.

corn fritters

hominy deluxe

Yield: 4 to 6 servings

    ½ **pound pork sausage**
    3 **cups canned hominy, drained**
    3 **tablespoons chopped onion**
    1 **cup canned tomato soup**
    ½ **teaspoon salt**
    ½ **cup seasoned bread or cracker crumbs**

In a medium-size skillet cook the pork sausage until the fat begins to come off it. Add the hominy and onion; cook until all are browned and blended. Add the tomato soup and salt; stir until hot.

To serve this, top the hot hominy with the seasoned bread crumbs. It looks hefty and tastes good, too.

skillet lettuce

Yield: 4 servings

    1 **head lettuce, cored and cut into quarters**
    ½ **cup beef stock**
    Salt to taste
    Melted butter to pour over the finished vegetable

Use a medium-size skillet with a top for this. Put the lettuce and beef stock into the skillet. Cover the skillet; cook lettuce over low heat 6 to 8 minutes. Most of the stock will be absorbed into the lettuce. Salt to taste, then pour melted butter over the lettuce. Serve it hot.

stuffed mushrooms

Yield: 6 to 8 servings

1 pound fresh white mushrooms
1 tablespoon chopped scallions
2 tablespoons butter
½ cup whipping cream

1 tablespoon sherry
1 teaspoon salt
¼ teaspoon freshly ground pepper
¼ cup fine bread crumbs

Remove stems from mushrooms; chop stems fine. Set caps aside.

Sauté mushroom stems and scallions in butter in medium-size skillet. Add cream, sherry, salt, pepper, and bread crumbs. Cook until liquid is absorbed and mixture fairly thick.

Fill each mushroom cap; put them on baking sheet. Broil at 375°F about 5 minutes or until bubbly.

If you want to make these ahead for company, freeze them before the final broiling. Then you will oven-cook them a little longer, until completely hot inside.

okay okra

Yield: 4 to 6 servings

2 tablespoons bacon fat or oil
1 large onion, sliced into rings
½ green pepper, chopped
2 cups canned tomatoes (1-pound can)
1 teaspoon salt
Dash of freshly ground pepper
1 teaspoon lemon juice or grated lemon rind
1 pound fresh okra, cut into 2-inch pieces
¼ cup flour
2 tablespoons oil
½ cup grated cheese

It takes 2 medium skillets to make this, but it's worth the extra trouble.

Start with the sauce. Heat the fat and tan the onion and green pepper in a skillet. Add tomatoes, salt, pepper, and lemon juice or rind. Simmer this 15 minutes.

Dust okra with flour. Prepare another skillet. Heat oil; add okra. Cook until heated but not brown. Reduce heat; pour sauce over okra. Add grated cheese; cover skillet. Simmer for 15 minutes. The okra will be tender and so okay.

onions for a party

Yield: 4 to 6 servings

4 tablespoons butter or margarine
2 pounds white onions, peeled
2 tablespoons dry white wine
3 cloves and ½ stick cinnamon
    tied in cheesecloth bag

1 cup beef broth
3 medium-size tomatoes, diced
½ teaspoon salt
½ teaspoon sugar

Melt butter in medium-sized, heavy skillet; brown the onions. This will take a few minutes of cooking. Add remaining ingredients; cover. Reduce heat to simmer; cook for 1 hour.

Remove spices, put onions in serving dish, and pour the pan juices over all.

beer fried onion ring

Yield: 4 to 6 servings

1½ cups flour
1½ cups beer

4 very large onions
Shortening for deep frying

Combine flour and beer in a large bowl, blending thoroughly with a wooden spoon. Cover bowl; keep at room temperature at least 3 hours.

Peel and slice onions into ¼-inch rounds. Divide into individual rings.

In large skillet heat enough shortening to drop in the onion rings. Dip a few onion rings at a time into prepared batter, then into hot oil. Fry until golden brown.

Place fried rings on a cookie sheet lined with paper towels. Keep warm in preheated 200°F oven.

These onion rings can be frozen and reheated in 400°F oven if desired.

beer fried onion rings

onions and green peppers

Yield: 4 servings

> 3 tablespoons butter or margarine
> 6 medium-size onions, peeled and sliced thin
> 3 whole green peppers, diced
> 2 tablespoons beef broth
> Salt and pepper to taste

Melt butter in medium skillet; sauté onions about 10 minutes. Add peppers; cook for 5 minutes more. Add beef broth and seasonings; cover. Simmer for 8 minutes more. Serve at once.

A variation of this is to add 2 whole diced tomatoes just before you cover the vegetables.

onion delight

This recipe starts in the skillet and ends in the oven—a good one to prepare for company, as it is easy on the cook.

Yield: 4 to 6 servings

> 6 large, mild onions, skinned and sliced
> 4 tablespoons bacon fat
> Salt and pepper to taste
> ½ cup bread crumbs
> ½ cup grated cheese
> Paprika for garnish

Sauté the onions in bacon fat in a medium-size skillet. When they are just tender but not browned, add salt and pepper to taste.

Place the onions in a shallow, greased baking dish. Sprinkle the top with bread crumbs, cheese, and paprika. Bake in a moderate 375°F oven until the topping is lightly browned.

frozen peas and beans with a fresh taste

From the taste of these vegetables, you'll think it's July even if the calendar says January.

Yield: 4 to 6 servings

1 package frozen green peas
1 package frozen cut green beans
4 tablespoons butter or margarine
½ cup blanched, sliced almonds (optional)

Remove the peas and beans from the freezer at least 1 hour before cooking.
Melt the butter in a medium-size skillet. Sauté the peas and beans in the butter for 3 to 5 minutes or until hot through. Stir in the sliced almonds; mix together gently.

caesar's vegetables

Serve this with your favorite steak. It's a winner.

Yield: 4 to 6 servings

3 to 4 onions, sliced in rings
3 to 4 medium potatoes, diced small into ¼-inch squares
¼ cup prepared Caesar's dressing

Prepare vegetables as indicated.
Heat the Caesar's dressing in a medium skillet. Add onions and potatoes. Stir over low heat several minutes. When onions are transparent, the dish is done. The potatoes will be crisp and all will have the well-seasoned flavor of the salad dressing.

dill new potatoes

Yield: 4 to 6 servings

24 small, whole new potatoes (canned may be used)
3 tablespoons butter or margarine
1 medium onion, chopped fine
1 teaspoon dillweed

Peel potatoes, or drain those in cans.

Heat butter in medium skillet; brown the chopped onion. Add more butter if needed. Put in potatoes; sprinkle with dillweed. Stir gently several times to thoroughly coat potatoes with butter and onions.

Put in a serving bowl and watch them go!

garlic potatoes

Yield: 4 to 6 servings

1 medium onion, chopped
1 small garlic clove, crushed
2 tablespoons olive oil
¾ cup chopped parsley
¼ cup chopped pimiento
1 teaspoon salt
Dash of pepper
1 cup chicken soup stock
4 to 6 medium potatoes, pared and sliced thin

In medium skillet place chopped onion and crushed garlic in heated olive oil, stirring until soft. Add parsley, pimiento, salt, pepper, and stock. When stock has come to a boil but not boiled, remove from heat.

Put potato slices into broth in layers. Return skillet to heat; bring to a boil. Cover; simmer potatoes 20 minutes or until tender to a fork.

potato balls

These are so good, the family will beg you to have leftover mashed potatoes so you can make them.

Yield: 4 to 6 servings

2 cups mashed potatoes
1 egg with 2 tablespoons water

Crushed cornflakes
Fat for deep frying

Shape the mashed potatoes into ice-cream-scoop balls. Roll each ball in the egg mixture, then in the crushed cornflakes.

Heat fat in a medium-size skillet. Fry the balls in the deep fat until nicely browned all over.

Put them on a warming platter until all are cooked, then watch them disappear at the table.

party sweet potatoes

Yield: 4 to 6 servings

About 2 cups mashed sweet potatoes
2 tablespoons melted butter
½ teaspoon salt
¼ teaspoon nutmeg
½ teaspoon cinnamon

¼ teaspoon ginger
1 cup chopped nuts
Flour
Fat for deep frying

Beat the sweet potatoes until they are light and fluffy. Add the butter and seasonings; mix well. Last, fold in the nuts. Shape this mixture into round balls about 2 inches in diameter. Roll each ball in flour.

Melt fat in a medium-size skillet. Drop the floured balls into the fat; cook them until light brown. Put the balls that are finished first on a warming platter until all are cooked and ready.

sweet-potato balls

Yield: 4 to 6 servings

½ teaspoon salt
Dash of pepper
2 cups mashed sweet potatoes
4 marshmallows

1 cup bread or cracker crumbs
1 egg, beaten
2 tablespoons water
Shortening for deep frying

Mix salt and pepper with sweet potatoes. Roll into 8 balls. Put 1 marshmallow into center of each ball. Roll each ball in dry crumbs.

Combine beaten egg and water. Dip balls into this mixture; roll them again in crumbs.

Fry in heated deep shortening about 4 minutes, until golden brown and crispy. Drain and serve.

potato pancakes with chives

Yield: 4 servings

2 tablespoons chopped chives
4 medium baked potatoes, grated
2 teaspoons salt
Several twists of freshly ground
    black pepper

1 tablespoon flour
2 tablespoons butter or margarine
2 tablespoons vegetable oil

Chop chives first; set aside.

Peel and grate potatoes coarsely into a large mixing bowl. Potatoes will accumulate potato water. Do not drain. Mix in chopped chives, salt, and pepper. Work as quickly as you can, so that potatoes do not turn brown. Add flour, mixing well.

Melt shortening in a large skillet. Drop potato mixture by spoonfuls into hot fat. The 3-inch pancakes will take about 3 minutes a side to become crisp and golden. Serve piping hot.

potato pancakes with chives

good fried rice

This can be made in the morning, put in a casserole, and reheated in the oven before serving.

Yield: 12 to 14 servings

3 cups uncooked rice
6 tablespoons oil
5 eggs, beaten
6 tablespoons soy sauce

¼ teaspoon garlic powder
2 onions, chopped
2 cups celery, sliced on diagonal

Cook rice until done; set aside to drain.

Heat oil in a large skillet. Pour beaten eggs into oil. As they harden, cut up eggs with 2 knives. Add soy sauce and garlic powder. Last, add cooked rice, onions, and celery. Stir over low heat 3 to 5 minutes or until all is well-blended.

good fried rice

mexican rice

Yield: 4 to 6 servings

        4 tablespoons oil
        1 small can mushrooms, drained
        1 medium onion, chopped
        1 green pepper, chopped
        2 cups canned tomatoes, drained
        ½ cup water or beef stock
        1 cup uncooked rice
        2 tablespoons chopped parsley
        1½ teaspoons salt
        Dash of pepper
        ½ teaspoon oregano

Heat oil in large skillet. Add mushrooms, onion, and green pepper; cook until onions are lightly tanned. Add tomatoes and water. When mixture has come to a boil, but not boiled, add rice and seasonings. Cover; simmer for 30 minutes, until rice is tender and most of the liquid has been absorbed.

rice and nut au gratin

Yield: 4 to 6 servings

        1 medium onion, minced fine
        1 green pepper, chopped
        3 tablespoons butter or margarine
        1 cup cooked rice
        ⅓ cup bread crumbs
        1 cup drained and chopped tomatoes
        1 cup chopped nutmeats
        1 beaten egg
        2 tablespoons chopped parsley
        1 teaspoon salt
        ¼ teaspoon paprika
        Grated cheese for topping

Sauté onion and green pepper in butter in a large skillet. When onion is transparent, add rice, bread crumbs, tomatoes, nuts, egg, parsley, salt, and paprika. Stir until all are well-blended. This will taste good just as is, but you're not finished yet.

Grease a 2-quart casserole dish. Put mixture from skillet into it. Sprinkle with grated cheese and bake at 350°F for 30 minutes.

thanksgiving rice

This holiday treat can be used in two ways—as a vegetable addition to the meal or as an unusual stuffing for the turkey. It can be made ahead, frozen, and reheated in the oven if desired. The large quantity makes it a versatile delicacy.

Yield: 2 large casseroles

>   3 cups uncooked rice
>   1 pound country sausage
>   1 cup chopped celery
>   2 medium onions, chopped
>   1 green pepper, diced
>   1 egg, beaten
>   Salt and pepper to taste

Boil rice first; set it aside in a colander.

Use a large skillet for this. Cook country sausage thoroughly. It will draw enough fat to sauté the celery, onions, and green pepper. When vegetables are tanned, not brown, add rice to mixture; stir well about 3 minutes. Remove to your largest bowl. Add beaten egg and seasonings; mix well.

Put rice in well-greased casseroles for serving or freezing. Reheat in oven just enough so that rice is hot.

sour-creamy sauerkraut

This is tasty enough to serve for company and easy enough that you will want to serve it often.

Yield: 4 to 6 servings

>   3 tablespoons butter, margarine, or oil
>   1 onion, chopped
>   1 pound sauerkraut, undrained
>   ½ teaspoon freshly ground black pepper
>   Salt to taste
>   4 tablespoons sour cream

Melt shortening in medium skillet and lightly brown onion. Add sauerkraut, stirring to mix; cover skillet. Simmer for 1 hour. Uncover pan. Drain off excess liquid. Add pepper and salt if needed. Just before serving, stir in sour cream.

skillet spinach

Skillet spinach is good because the vegetable is not overcooked.

Yield: 4 to 6 servings

>2 tablespoons oil
>1 pound loose fresh spinach, washed and drained
>½ teaspoon salt
>½ teaspoon garlic salt
>¼ teaspoon sugar

Heat oil in large skillet. Add spinach, stirring with a wooden spoon until leaves are oil-coated. Cover; cook just 1 minute. Uncover skillet; sprinkle spinach with seasonings. Stir; cook for 30 seconds more, until spinach leaves are just wilted.

fried green tomatoes

This is an excellent way to use a bumper crop of tomatoes that has not ripened fast enough. Green tomatoes go well with corn on the cob—a true summer delight.

Yield: 4 to 6 servings

>4 medium green tomatoes, sliced ½ inch thick
>1 teaspoon salt
>½ teaspoon pepper
>1 teaspoon dillweed
>1 cup cornmeal
>Fat for frying

Wash and prepare tomatoes—and these must be green.
Mix seasonings with cornmeal in a pie plate. Batter each tomato slice, being sure both sides are coated.
Heat fat in medium skillet; cook tomatoes until brown on both sides. Drain on paper towels.

skillet summer squash

Yield: 4 to 6 servings

4 tablespoons oil
1 large onion, chopped
1½ pounds summer squash, cubed
1 tomato, cut in wedges (optional)

1 teaspoon salt
¼ teaspoon ground pepper
¼ teaspoon dillweed or
  fresh dill

Heat oil in medium skillet; cook onion until soft. Add squash, tomato, and seasonings. Cover skillet; cook for 10 minutes. Do not allow squash to get mushy. Overcooking will spoil the dish.

skillet salad

Yield: 4 to 6 servings

1 large bowl of fresh greens
  (collard, mustard, spinach,
  turnip, or beet)

6 to 8 slices bacon
1 tablespoon vinegar
1 cup seasoned croutons

Wash and dry greens; chop or cut them up into a large salad bowl.
In a medium skillet fry bacon crisp; drain slices. Break bacon slices into bits.
Add vinegar to fat left in skillet; stir until hot. Pour mixture over salad greens so that greens wilt. Add croutons; toss again. The salad is ready to eat.

fried zucchini

Yield: 4 to 6 servings

3 to 4 large zucchini, sliced
  into rounds
1 egg
1 tablespoon milk

3 tablespoons flour
1 teaspoon salt
1 teaspoon garlic salt
Deep fat for frying

Wash and slice zucchini into rounds about ¼ inch thick. Set aside.
Combine egg, milk, flour, salt, and garlic salt in a bowl. Mix well to form batter. Dip each zucchini round into batter; fry in deep fat. Batter zucchini as you are ready to fry it, so each piece is coated. Fry until crisp and golden brown. Drain on paper towels. Serve hot.

zucchini italian

Yield: 4 servings

    2 tablespoons butter or shortening
    1 onion, sliced into rings
    1 pound zucchini, sliced (2 to 3 cups)
    1 cup diced fresh tomatoes
    1 teaspoon salt
    Dash of pepper
    1 teaspoon dillweed

Heat butter in medium skillet. Use skillet with its own top. Cook onion rings in butter until yellow. Add zucchini, tomatoes, salt, pepper, and dillweed. Cover; lower heat to simmer. Cook for 10 to 15 minutes, until vegetables are tender.

If you want this for company and want to make it ahead, put the cooked vegetables in a casserole dish and sprinkle with grated cheese. Just before serving, put into moderate oven for 5 minutes or until cheese has browned.

zucchini

summer delight

Yield: 4 to 6 servings

⅓ cup olive oil
2 or 3 large onions, chopped fine
2 medium zucchini, washed and cubed
2 green peppers, coarsely chopped
2 teaspoons salt
3 fresh ripe tomatoes or 2 cups canned tomatoes, drained

Heat olive oil in a large skillet that has its own top. Add onions, zucchini, green peppers, and salt. Stir once or twice to blend; cover. Simmer about 40 minutes.

While this is cooking, put fresh tomatoes in a saucepan; cook until soft. Stir and mash them slightly. If canned tomatoes are used, break them into pieces. Add tomatoes to skillet; cook just 5 minutes more, until flavors are blended.

These are delicious served hot but are just as good served as a cold vegetable if leftover.

Using the same recipe, try 1 teaspoon dillweed or 1 teaspoon oregano. This makes a good variation.

hot vegetable symphony

Yield: 4 to 6 servings

The true yield of this recipe depends on what you put into the skillet. Use a combination of vegetables that appeals to you and is plentiful in season.

Start with carrots. Dice fine, garden-fresh carrots. Slice onions, zucchini, squash, green peppers, and so forth. Prepare enough vegetables for your family's needs.

Put carrots in heavy skillet; add just enough water to cover them. When carrots have come to a boil, add onions; cook about 1 minute. Add rest of vegetables; simmer very slowly 3 to 5 minutes. Season with salt, pepper, and a little lemon juice. Serve hot at once, or chill for a salad if preferred.

dinner in the skillet

macaroni and beef dinner

Yield: 4 to 6 servings

    1 cup elbow macaroni
    1 pound lean ground beef
    2 medium onions, diced
    1 clove garlic, mashed fine
    2 tablespoons oil
    1 8-ounce can tomato sauce
    1 teaspoon salt
    ¼ teaspoon black pepper
    1 cup catsup
    1 can mushrooms (optional)
    2 tablespoons Worcestershire sauce
    ½ teaspoon oregano

Cook macaroni according to package directions; drain.

In medium skillet sauté meat, onions, and garlic in oil. Add rest of ingredients in order given. Bring to a boil, then simmer for a few minutes. Add cooked macaroni; simmer for 5 minutes more. Serve at once.

busy-day rice ragout

see p. 131

This fast put-together makes hearty eating.

Yield: 4 to 6 servings

(more double) 1 small onion, chopped
1 green pepper, chopped
1 tablespoon oil
1 pound lean ground beef or veal
1 teaspoon salt
Dash of black pepper

1 tablespoon prepared mustard
2 tablespoons catsup
1 tablespoon Worcestershire sauce
(1) 3 cups cooked rice
3 cups canned tomatoes — _Polly-O (28 oz) crushed_

Use a medium to large skillet. Stir onion and green pepper in oil until soft. Add ground meat, salt, and pepper; stir until meat loses its pink color. Add remaining ingredients; stir until well-blended. Reduce heat; cover skillet. Simmer just 15 minutes.

While the ragout is simmering, toss a salad and sit down to eat relaxed after a busy day.

busy-day rice ragout

spinach and beef delight

Yield: 4 to 6 servings

1 medium onion, chopped
6 mushrooms, sliced
1 pound ground beef
2 tablespoons shortening
1 10-ounce package frozen chopped spinach
1 cup sour cream
2 cups creamed cottage cheese
½ teaspoon oregano
1 teaspoon dillweed
1 teaspoon salt
1 teaspoon garlic salt
½ teaspoon freshly ground black pepper

Brown onion, mushrooms, and beef in shortening in a medium-sized, deep skillet. Stir until meat loses its pink color. Add frozen spinach as is. Cook uncovered on medium heat until spinach has thawed and some of the liquid is absorbed. Stir in sour cream and cottage cheese, mixing until all is heated but not boiling. Add seasonings; mix well. Let skillet stand until ready to serve.

Return skillet to heat for 2 or 3 minutes just before dinner is ready. Serve with French bread and a salad.

sausage and apple casserole

Yield: 4 to 6 servings

8 cups cubed white bread (about 15 slices)
1 pound country sausage
1 large onion, diced
1 green pepper, diced
½ cup water
2 large apples, pared, cored,
  and chopped
1 teaspoon salt

Use stale white bread for cubes, or stale them by putting in 250°F oven for 10 minutes.

Brown the country sausage in a large skillet. Cook until there is no trace of pink in meat. Add onion and green pepper; cook for 2 minutes more. Stir in bread cubes, water, apples, and salt. Mix together until all is evenly moist.

Turn out cooked mixture into a well-greased casserole. Cook in 350°F oven 30 minutes or until the top crusts.

Since this is a meal in itself, all you will need with it is a large tossed salad.

tomato ground beef

tomato ground beef

Yield: 4 to 6 servings

    1 tablespoon shortening
    1 large onion, diced
    1 green pepper, diced
    1½ pounds ground beef
    1 carrot, diced
    1 can tomato soup
    1 teaspoon salt
    1 teaspoon garlic salt
    ¼ teaspoon freshly ground black pepper

Heat shortening in medium skillet; tan the onion and green pepper. Add beef and diced carrot. Sauté for 1 minute. Add can of soup without diluting; add seasonings. Simmer about 5 minutes to blend flavors.

To make this a complete meal, add 1 cup of cooked rice, or serve over cooked noodles or spaghetti. This is another quick-and-easy meal.

129

sausage, cabbage, and rice

Yield: 4 to 6 servings

> 1 pound country sausage
> 1 small head cabbage, shredded
> ½ cup uncooked rice
> 2 teaspoons dillweed
> 1 cup chicken broth
> 1 teaspoon salt
> ¼ teaspoon pepper

Brown the country sausage in large skillet. It will render enough fat to cook remaining ingredients. Add shredded cabbage; stir until cabbage is thoroughly coated with fat. Add rest of ingredients in order given. Cover skillet; cook on low heat 25 minutes or until rice is done.

Complete the dinner with a big plate of raw vegetables.

chicken-in-a-pot dinner

Yield: 4 to 6 servings

> 3 tablespoons butter or margarine
> 1 2½- to 3-pound frying chicken, cut into serving pieces
> Salt and pepper to taste
> ¾ cup chicken broth
> 6 to 8 mushrooms, sliced (optional)
> 1 1-pound can whole potatoes, drained
> 1 medium onion, sliced into rings
> 1 teaspoon salt
> ½ teaspoon paprika
> 1 10-ounce package frozen peas, thawed
> 4 tomatoes, quartered

Heat butter in a large skillet; brown the chicken pieces. Add salt and pepper while cooking. Add chicken broth, cover skillet, and simmer for 30 minutes. Add mushrooms, potatoes, onion rings, salt, and paprika; cook for 5 minutes more, adding ¼ cup chicken broth if needed. Last, add peas and tomatoes; cook for a few minutes more, until chicken and vegetables are heated through.

Serve with your favorite hot bread.

veal and rice skillet dinner

Yield: 4 to 6 servings

1 pound ground veal
2 green peppers, chopped
1 cup sliced onion
1 cup uncooked rice

1 can beef broth plus
1 cup water (totaling 2½ cups liquid)
1 tablespoon soy sauce

Brown the veal in medium skillet until all pink disappears. Add remaining ingredients. Allow to come to a boil, but do not boil. Reduce heat; cover. Cook for 25 minutes.

Dinner is done—delicious, too.

chicken dinner with asparagus

This is one of those recipes that takes longer to read than actually to do. It goes together easily and is so good.

3 whole chicken breasts, boned,
    skinned, and cut into strips
    1½ inches long
6 tablespoons vegetable oil
8 to 10 stalks fresh asparagus,
    cleaned and cut into
    1½ inch lengths
1 cup chopped green onions
1 3- or 4-ounce can sliced
    mushrooms with liquid

1 can condensed chicken broth
1½ teaspoons ground ginger
1 teaspoon salt
1 teaspoon sugar
½ teaspoon garlic salt
2 tablespoons cornstarch
⅓ cup dry sherry
3 tablespoons soy sauce
4 cups cooked rice

In large skillet sauté chicken strips in 4 tablespoons oil until meat turns white. Remove from skillet; keep chicken warm.

Heat remaining oil in skillet; add asparagus and onions. Stir for 2 minutes. Add chicken, mushrooms, broth, and seasonings. Stir, cover, and simmer for 3 minutes.

Mix cornstarch with sherry and soy sauce to make a smooth paste. (Water may be used instead of wine if preferred.) Add to skillet; stir until mixture thickens slightly.

Serve over hot rice.

fast fish dinner

Yield: 4 servings

    2 cups canned tomatoes, drained (1-pound can)
    2 tablespoons butter or margarine
    1½ cups diced celery
    2 medium onions, sliced
    1 pound frozen fish fillets, cut into bite-size pieces
    1 teaspoon salt
    ¼ teaspoon black pepper
    2 cups canned potatoes, drained and sliced
    Parsley for garnish

Put drained tomatoes and butter in medium skillet; bring to a boil. Add celery and onions; simmer until onions are soft, 3 to 5 minutes. Add fish, salt, pepper, and potatoes, stirring once. Cover skillet; simmer this 10 minutes.

Garnish with parsley, and serve.

fast fish dinner

hartshorns

This is a two-part recipe, but is worth the trouble, since hartshorns store well and can be made ahead.

Yield: 36 hartshorns

¼ pound butter or margarine
4 eggs
1 cup sugar
½ lemon rind, grated

½ teaspoon ground cardamom
2 teaspoons baking soda
4½ cups flour
Fat for deep frying

Melt butter and allow to cool.

Beat eggs and sugar together. Add butter, lemon rind, cardamom, baking soda, and flour. Mix well; place in refrigerator to chill overnight.

Roll small lumps of dough into strips 6 inches long and as thick as your little finger. Form each strip into a ring. Cook rings in deep fat until golden brown. Drain well on paper towels; store in a sealed tin.

grandmother cookies

Grandmother mixes these cookies, but little hands can help shape them. Fun for everybody. Eat these all up—they're too good to store.

Yield: 3 dozen plus

½ cup margarine
½ cup sugar
2 eggs
2 cups flour

2 teaspoons baking powder
1 teaspoon salt
1½ teaspoons cinnamon
½ cup raisins (optional)

Cream together margarine, sugar, and eggs until smooth.

Combine dry ingredients; add to egg mixture. Last, add raisins if desired. Batter will be stiff and buttery.

Take a teaspoonful, roll it between your palms, and flatten it to the size of a 2-inch circle. Put into lightly greased skillet. When cookie puffs up, turn it once and brown the other side.

christmas crullers

christmas crullers

These crullers are keepers and can be made well ahead of when needed and stored in a tin. They keep—if you can keep fingers out of the tin. They are so good.

Yield: About 36 crullers

3 eggs
⅓ cup sugar
⅔ cup butter or margarine, melted
¼ teaspoon ground cardamom
Grated rind of 1 lemon

3 tablespoons cream
4 cups flour
Shortening for deep frying
Powdered sugar for topping

Beat eggs and sugar together until very light. Stir in melted butter, cardamom, and lemon rind. Add cream and flour. The dough will be quite buttery and easy to handle.

Roll out dough about ¼ inch thick. Cut with pastry cutter or knife into oblongs 1 inch wide. Cut a slit into the middle of each oblong and pull one corner through to make a knot. If you prefer, just twist the oblong to make a ribbon effect.

Heat fat in skillet. Fry crullers until lightly browned; drain on paper. Store in a tightly covered container.

When ready to serve, sprinkle with powdered sugar.

doughnut drops

Yield: 2 dozen or more

2 eggs, beaten
¼ cup sugar
1 teaspoon salt
2 tablespoons melted butter or margarine
1½ cups flour

4 teaspoons baking powder
⅓ cup milk
Fat for deep frying
Cinnamon-sugar for topping

Mix eggs, sugar, salt, and melted butter in a bowl. Add flour, baking powder, and milk, stirring all with a wooden spoon until dough is formed. It will be thin enough to drop from a tablespoon.

Heat fat in skillet. Drop mixture by tablespoons into hot fat. Cook until browned all over. Remove; drain on paper towels.

Sprinkle with cinnamon and sugar mixture.

chocolate doughnut drops

If you want chocolate doughnut drops, add 1 ounce of melted chocolate to the dough.

sweet-potato doughnuts

Yield: About 30 doughnuts

2 eggs, beaten
¾ cup sugar
3 tablespoons butter or margarine
¾ cup mashed cooked
    sweet potatoes
¼ cup milk
3½ cups flour

4 teaspoons double-acting
    baking powder
½ teaspoon salt
¼ teaspoon nutmeg
¼ teaspoon cinnamon
Fat for deep frying
Sugar and cinnamon for topping

Using your mixer, mix eggs, sugar, butter, and sweet potatoes in a large bowl. Add milk.

Sift together dry ingredients; add to the bowl. When well-mixed, set bowl in refrigerator to chill, at least 1 hour.

On floured board roll out dough to ½ inch thickness. Cut with either a doughnut cutter or a floured glass with rim measuring 3 inches.

In skillet heat fat for deep frying. When hot enough, drop in doughnuts; cook them until golden brown all around. Drain doughnuts on paper towels.

Sprinkle with sugar and cinnamon, and enjoy.

sour-cream doughnuts I

Yield: 2½ to 3 dozen

    3 eggs, slightly beaten
    1¼ cups sugar
    1 cup sour cream
    4 plus cups flour
    2 teaspoons baking powder
    1 teaspoon baking soda
    1 teaspoon nutmeg
    ½ teaspoon salt
    Fat for deep frying
    Sugar mixed with cinnamon

Beat eggs and sugar in a large bowl. Add sour cream.

Sift together dry ingredients; gradually add to egg mixture. When mixture has formed a dough, allow to rest 15 minutes.

Roll out dough on a well-floured board. Cut with floured doughnut cutter, the hole too; set aside. The cut doughnuts will rest 15 minutes more.

Drop doughnuts into preheated deep fat; cook until evenly browned.

Roll the hot cooked doughnuts in sugar mixed with cinnamon.

sour-cream doughnuts I

sour-cream doughnuts II

These will go fast.

Yield: 30 or more doughnuts

3 eggs
1 cup sugar
1 teaspoon baking soda
1 cup sour cream
3¼ cups flour

1 teaspoon nutmeg
1 teaspoon salt
Fat for deep frying
Confectioners' sugar for topping

Beat eggs and sugar together.

Mix soda with sour cream; add to egg mixture. Gradually add flour, nutmeg, and salt. When all flour is absorbed, cover dough; put in refrigerator overnight.

Roll out dough on a floured board to ¼ inch thickness. Cut with doughnut cutter or into desired shapes.

Heat fat in skillet; drop doughnuts into fat. Doughnuts are done when lightly browned all around. Drain on paper towels.

Dust with confectioners' sugar.

snowballs

This old family recipe makes a delicious cookie confection that melts in the mouth. It takes a bit of time but is worth it for the taste. These store well if you can keep the family from eating them.

Yield: A large, full cookie tin

2 eggs
1 egg shell of water (about 3 tablespoons)
1 teaspoon salt

2 cups sifted flour
Fat for deep frying
Confectioners' sugar

In a large bowl beat eggs, water, and salt with a fork. Add flour gradually until dough is sticky.

Knead gently on a floured board until dough can be easily handled. Divide dough into 4 round balls; let stand 1 hour.

Roll out dough as thin as you can. Let stand rolled out 30 minutes or until dry.

Cut dough into 3-inch squares or triangles (or some of each).

Heat fat in deep skillet; drop snowballs into hot fat. They cook quickly. When golden brown, remove from fat; drain on paper towels.

Sprinkle them liberally with confectioners' sugar.

easy chocolate crepes

Crepes are both easy and fun to make. The mixing is a snap.

Yield: 18 to 24 crepes

> 2 eggs
> ½ cup flour
> 2 tablespoons cocoa
> ¼ cup sugar
> 1 cup milk plus 2 tablespoons cream
> 1 teaspoon vanilla
> 1 tablespoon butter, melted and cooled

Place eggs in a bowl. Add remaining ingredients in order given and beat well, by twos—mix flour and cocoa; beat; sugar and milk; beat; vanilla and cooled butter; beat. Set batter aside for at least 1 hour.

Heat a small skillet or crepe pan. Brush very lightly with butter. Place 1 tablespoon crepe batter into pan. Pick up pan by its handle and swirl batter so it covers the edges. This is fun. Cook just 1 minute, then turn. These cook quickly. (One recipe suggests you turn crepes with fingers, not with a lift. It works, too.) When done, remove to paper towels.

Fill and enjoy, or store in freezer for the future.

dessert pancakes with fruit

This is a picture dessert that tastes as good as it looks.

Yield: 4 to 6 servings

> 1 cup prepared pancake mix
> 1 4-ounce package butterscotch
>   pudding mix
> 1 cup milk
> 2 eggs, beaten
>
> 2 tablespoons oil
> Oil for lightly greased skillet
> ½ cup sour cream
> 2 packages frozen fruit, thawed

Combine pancake mix, pudding, milk, eggs, and oil in a bowl. Beat with rotary beater or spoon until batter is even.

Heat a lightly greased medium skillet. Drop in batter 1 tablespoon at a time. When golden on the bottom, turn with a spatula; allow to cook until both sides are golden. Keep cooked pancakes warm.

When ready to serve, arrange several pancakes per plate. Top with a spoonful of sour cream and spoon over the thawed fruit.

apple rings

Yield: 12 or more rings

3 or 4 large apples
2 eggs, separated
2 teaspoons sugar
¼ teaspoon salt
¼ teaspoon ground cardamom

2 tablespoons butter, melted
¾ cup milk
1 cup flour
Shortening for deep frying

Peel, core, and slice apples ½ inch thick.

Beat egg whites stiff; set aside.

Beat egg yolks; add sugar, salt, and cardamom. Add melted butter, milk, and flour. Beat thoroughly. Fold in stiffened egg whites.

Dip a slice of apple into batter; drop at once into hot deep fat. Fry until lightly browned. Drain apples, put them on serving platter, and sprinkle with sugar. Serve them warm.

brown betty with hard sauce

Yield: 4 to 6 servings

4 cups cinnamon-raisin bread cubes
4 tablespoons butter or margarine
½ cup brown sugar
1 jar or can applesauce (2 cups)
½ teaspoon cinnamon
½ teaspoon salt

In medium skillet sauté bread cubes in melted butter. When lightly browned, add sugar, applesauce, cinnamon, and salt. Stir until hot.

Serve warm with a dollop of hard sauce on top.

hard sauce

2 tablespoons soft butter or margarine
½ cup confectioners' sugar
½ teaspoon lemon or orange rind

Mix ingredients together in order given in a bowl until hard sauce is very smooth. It will melt into the warm Brown Betty and be mouth-watering good.

bananas flambé

Yield: 4 servings

4 tablespoons butter or margarine
2 tablespoons brown sugar
1 teaspoon cinnamon
6 peeled ripe bananas, cut in half lengthwise
¼ cup rum

Melt butter in medium skillet.

Mix brown sugar and cinnamon; sprinkle some of this over cut bananas.

Put bananas in butter on a moderate to low heat; cook until lightly browned. Turn once and sprinkle with remaining sugar mixture. Last, add rum.

You can play French chef and ignite this for a glamour dessert. Serve bananas by themselves or over vanilla ice cream.

bananas flambé

peaches in wine sauce

This can be made in a saucepan, but a heavy skillet with a lid preserves all the syrup.

Yield: 8 servings

  8 ripe peaches
  ¾ cup sugar
  ⅓ cup water
  ⅓ cup white wine

Scald and peel skins off peaches, leaving fruit whole.

Combine sugar and water in medium skillet; cook for 5 minutes. Add peaches; simmer for 5 minutes more. Add wine; simmer again for 5 minutes. Five minutes cooking time is usually enough to make fruit tender and syrup slightly thickened. Baste 3 times while cooking.

Transfer cooked peaches to a bowl; cover with the syrup. Refrigerate; serve when chilled.

rum rice dessert

Yield: 4 to 6 servings

  ¼ cup raisins
  ¼ cup rum
  1 cup uncooked rice
  1 teaspoon salt
  1 cup sugar
  3 cups milk
  2 tablespoons chopped nuts
  1 teaspoon lemon juice
  1 egg, beaten
  ¼ pound butter or margarine
  Cinnamon and sugar mixed together

The night before, or at least several hours ahead, soak raisins in rum.

In top part of double boiler or in very heavy saucepan, cook rice, salt, sugar, and milk 30 minutes. Rice will be tender and the liquid absorbed. To this add raisins, nuts, lemon juice, and beaten egg.

Melt butter in a medium skillet. Do not let butter brown. Add rice mixture; cook until it is crusty on edges. Then turn rice so that other side browns, too.

When ready to serve, sprinkle with cinnamon-sugar. Mmmmm. Good.

index